Maria's Mixes

A How-To Guide on Making Your Own Herbal Teas

©Copyright 2011 Maria Yeager
All rights reserved

No part of this book may be reproduced or transmitted in any form or by any means, electronic or mechanical, including photocopying, recording, or by any information storage and retrieval system, without the written permission of the author and except where permitted by law.

ISBN-13:
978-1508481829

ISBN-10:
1508481822

Printed in the United States of America

Cover design by Victor Rook – author, filmmaker, photographer, and web designer. His nature film *Beyond the Garden Gate* ran on PBS for four years and is the winner of two Telly Awards.

Important Notice
The statements in this book have not been evaluated by the U.S. Food and Drug Administration. The herbs and teas in this book are not intended to diagnose, treat, cure or prevent any disease. The author accepts no responsibility for any illness or harm as a result of the use or misuse of the plants/herbs described in this book.

For my mom
Thanks for all the help with editing this book and all your support with Maria's Mixes!

Table of Contents

Preface..9

A word of caution…..11

Common Plant and Herbal Terms..13

Tips on How to Make Herbal Teas...15

Herbs/Foods Used in the Recipes...17

    Allspice (*Pimenta dioica*) _____ 19

    Catnip (*Nepeta cataria*) _____ 20

    Cayenne Pepper (*Capsicum frutescens*, also *Capsicum minimum*) _____ 22

    Chamomile (*Matriacaria recutita*) _____ 23

    Cinnamon (*Cinnamomum zeylanicum*) _____ 25

    Cleavers (*Galium aparine*) _____ 26

    Clove (*Syzygium aromaticum*, also *Eugenia aromaticum*, *Eugenia caryophyllata*) _____ 28

    Cramp Bark (*Viburnum opulus*) _____ 29

    Cranberry (*Vaccinium macrocarpon*) _____ 31

    Cornsilk (*Zea Mays*) _____ 32

    Dandelion (*Taraxacum officinale*) _____ 34

    Echinacea (*Echinacea purpurea*, also *Echinacea augustifolia*, *Rudbeckia purpurea*) _____ 35

    Fennel Seed (*Foeniculum vulgare*) _____ 37

    Ginger (*Zingiber officinale*) _____ 39

    Gingko (*Gingko biloba*) _____ 40

    Ginseng (*Panax ginseng*) _____ 42

    Goji Berry (*Lycium barbarum*, also *Lycium chinense*) _____ 44

    Goldenseal (*Hydrastis canadensis*) _____ 45

    Hibiscus (*Hibiscus rosa-sinensis*) _____ 47

    Hops (*Humulus lupulus*) _____ 49

    Lavender (*Lavandula augustifolia*, also *Lavandula officinalis*, *Lavandula spica*, *Lavandula vera*) _____ 51

    Lemon Balm (*Melissa officinalis*) _____ 52

    Lemon Grass (*Cymbopogon citratus*) _____ 54

    Lemon Peel (*Citrus limon*) _____ 55

Licorice Root (*Glycyrrhiza glabra*) 57
Marshmallow (*Althaea officinalis*) 58
Milk Thistle (*Silybum marianum*, also *Carduus benedictus, Carduus marianus*) 60
Nettle (*Urtica dioica*, also *Urtica urens*) 61
Nutmeg (*Myristica fragrans*) 63
Orange Peel (*Citrus sinensis*) 64
Parsley (*Petroselinum crispum*) 66
Passionflower (*Passiflora incarnate*) 67
Peppermint (*Mentha piperita*, also *Mentha nigricans*) 69
Rose Hips (*Rosa rugosa, Rosa acicularis, Rosa cinnamomea, Rosa canina*) 70
Rosemary (*Rosemarinus officinalis*) 72
Spearmint (*Mentha spicata*, also *Mentha crispa* or *Mentha* 74
Skullcap (*Scutellaria lateriflora*) 75
Slippery Elm Bark (*Ulmus rubra* or *Ulmus fulva*) 77
Uva Ursi (*Arctostaphylos uva-ursi*) 78
Wild Yam (*Dioscorea villosa*) 80

Maria's Mixes Herbal Tea Recipes 83

About Maria's Mixes, LLC 84

Ginger, Fennel and Peppermint 86
Rose Hips and Orange Peel 87
Chamomile, Hops and Catnip 88
The Perfect Blend 89
Lemon Balm and Chamomile 90
Brady's Blend 91
Milk Thistle and Allspice 92
Cranberry and Allspice Autumn Blend 93
Santa's Christmas Mint Tea 94
Jefferson Tea 95
Lullaby Lemon 96
Passionflower and Chamomile 97
Echinacea and Cinnamon 98
Refreshing Mint Sun Tea 99

Recommended Companies for Herbal Tea Supplies 101

Quick Herb vs. Diseases/Disorder Charts 107

About the Charts... 108

    CARDIOVASCULAR DISEASES/DISORDERS 109

    DIGESTIVE DISEASES/DISORDERS 110

    EYE/EAR/MOUTH DISEASES/DISORDERS 112

    GALLBLADDER/LIVER/PANCREAS DISEASES/DISORDERS 113

    IMMUNE SYSTEM DISEASES/DISORDERS 114

    MISCELLANEOUS DISEASES/DISORDERS 115

    MUSCULOSKELETAL DISEASES/DISORDERS 116

    NEUROLOGICAL DISEASES/DISORDERS 117

    REPRODUCTIVE DISEASES/DISORDERS 118

    RESPIRATORY TRACT DISEASES/DISORDERS 119

    SKIN DISEASES/DISORDERS 120

    URINARY TRACT DISEASES/DISORDERS 121

References 123

Index... 125

Acknowledgements 131

About the Author... 133

Preface

Photo by Dave O via Flickr/Creative Commons

Ah, the relaxing moments of enjoying the aroma and taste of a nice cup of herbal tea! Just getting up in the morning and having something tasty and hot to start off your day is such a great feeling whether you are busy or not. What is even better is that drinking herbal tea can actually be good for you! Herbs are loaded with vitamins, minerals, volatile oils and other constituents that work with your body to support optimal health.

I first became interested in nutrition and herbs when I was going through my own personal health crisis. My first positive experience was when I started using omega 3 fatty acids on a regular basis and saw a dramatic reduction in my symptoms. As I studied more about holistic nutrition, I came to realize that herbs are actually very powerful substances that play a very important role in overall health. Although herbs cannot "cure" an illness, they give your body extra support so you have what I refer to as "a suit of armor" in fighting disease. Due to all of the toxins and microbiological assaults that we are subject to every day, I believe it is in our best interest to arm our bodies with as much "armor" as we can get!

I am, however, also a scientist. I have a bachelor's degree in microbiology and have worked in the fields of microbiology and genetics for nearly 25 years. About 20 years ago, I would have laughed at someone who claimed that herbs had much of a benefit in improving overall health. However, I have come to realize the powerful benefits herbs have to offer. I believe I offer a different perspective on the use of herbs because I also have such a strong science background. Although I do believe in the power of herbs, I do not believe herbs should be relied on entirely for optimum health. There are circumstances where medication is necessary in the treatment of disease. Herbs are, in my opinion, a great addition to a healthy lifestyle. For example, if a person is healthy without any signs of a urinary tract infection but is interested in keeping the kidneys and urinary tract in good health, drinking an herbal tea containing herbs that promote the health of the urinary tract would be an excellent addition to his or her diet. However, if someone has a raging urinary tract infection, a physician should be seen immediately. Solely drinking herbal tea in this situation is not advised. The infection may need to be treated with antibiotics, and although herbal use in this situation may help support the urinary tract, it may not be strong enough to treat the infection.

The teas in this book were developed with a specific disease condition in mind; however, these teas should not be expected to "cure" any condition. They are meant as an adjunct to medical treatment to help arm our bodies so they can better fight the condition. One person who tried one of my teas while fighting a cold made the comment that the tea was very tasty and she really enjoyed it, but she didn't feel any better after drinking it. One cup of tea will not make the cold go away or make much difference in the way a person feels. Continual use of the tea, however, may support the immune system and help the person fight the cold more effectively. These teas are not meant as a "quick cure".

The first section of this book gives a short description of the herbs used in Maria's Mixes recipes. It is a good idea to review these descriptions before making and consuming any of the teas in this book, especially if you are on any medications as the herbs may interfere with their activity. The second section is the actual Maria's Mixes recipes with a short explanation as to what body system is being targeted. I certainly hope you enjoy this book and, more importantly, the herbal tea recipes!

A word of caution…

Photo by Dave O via Flickr/Creative Commons

As you read through this book, you will notice cautions and a list of known medication interactions with each of the herbs listed. Although very small amounts of these herbs are used in the herbal teas, please take these warnings very seriously. If you have any kind of chronic health condition or are taking any prescription medication, please consult your physician before using these herbs.

About half of all prescription medications currently on the market today are based on plant constituents. Prescription medications, however, are much more concentrated than the original herb. Therefore, these drugs are also much more likely to cause side effects. Additionally, herbs are generally weaker than the concentrated drugs and will take longer to work. Salicin, which has anti-inflammatory properties, is the active ingredient in white willow bark. Aspirin, or salicylic acid, is made from salicin. Large amounts of aspirin can cause stomach bleeding, but white willow bark is weaker and less likely to have this side effect although it would take longer to work. It would be inadvisable to combine aspirin and white willow bark because the combined effect of the salicylates would greatly increase the chances of stomach bleeding.

Although most herbs are generally harmless unless taken in very large quantities, there are exceptions to this rule. One example of a particularly dangerous plant is foxglove. Foxglove is a member of the *Digitalis* genus of plants and contains a cardiac glycoside called digoxen. This substance is used to make any of the digitalin group of drugs with one example being Lanoxin. These are valuable cardiac drugs; however, the plant itself can be quite dangerous if consumed. Symptoms of overdose of digoxen include nausea, vomiting, diarrhea, convulsions, disturbances of heart rhythm and heart attack. Since serious effects may occur from consuming this plant, foxglove is also referred to as "Dead Man's Bells" or "Witches Gloves". Then there are other herbs, such as comfrey, which contain active substances that are so controversial that there are legal restrictions on their use. Comfrey contains pyrrolizioline alkaloids which in some studies have shown that they may be carcinogenic; however, other studies have not confirmed this association.

As you read through this book, you will see possible drug interactions for each herb. It is very important to familiarize yourself with these interactions. Licorice, for example, is a wonderful adaptogenic and tasty herb; however, it can pose some serious health risks to anyone with high blood pressure, kidney disease or heart disease. Licorice taken over a long period of time (4 to 6 weeks) can lower potassium levels and increase sodium levels in the body. This can lead to increased blood pressure, water retention and heart problems. Therefore, it is inadvisable to use this herb if you are on digoxin, diuretics or medications for high blood pressure. Another example is dandelion. Because of its powerful diuretic effect, this herb should not be consumed if you are currently taking a prescription diuretic.

As you can see, it is a really good idea to educate yourself on each herb that you intend to consume to avoid any possible side effects or drug interactions. In this book, I have listed the herbs used in my herbal tea recipes. Included in the description of each herb are cautions on its use as well as known interactions with specific medications. Please familiarize yourself with the details of each herb prior to consuming these herbal teas.

Common Plant and Herbal Terms

Abortifacient – an herb which causes an abortion to occur
Adaptogen – an herb that improves resistance to stress
Alterative - an herb that detoxifies and increases vitality
Anesthetic – an herb that causes loss of sensation in a body part
Analgesic – an herb that relieves pain
Annual – a plant that flowers and dies in one season
Antibacterial – an herb that inhibits the growth of bacteria
Anthelmintic – an herb that destroys intestinal worms; see also vermifuge
Anticatarrhal – an herb that suppresses the buildup of phlegm
Anticonvulsant – an herb that is helpful in the treatment of seizures
Antifungal – an herb that destroys fungi or inhibits their growth
Antihistamine – an herb that counteracts the action of histamine which results in a reduction in the allergic response
Anti-inflammatory – an herb that reduces inflammation
Antimicrobial – an herb that destroys microorganisms
Antioxidant – an herb that inhibits oxidation and protects cells from damage
Antiparasitic – an herb that kills parasites
Antipyretic – an herb that reduces a fever
Antiseptic – an herb that controls or prevents infection
Antispasmodic – an herb that reduces muscle spasm
Antiviral – an herb that destroys viruses or inhibits their growth
Aperient – an herb that is a mild laxative
Aphrodisiac – an herb that stimulates sexual excitation
Astringent – an herb that reduces bleeding or discharge by precipitating proteins from the surfaces of cells
Biennial – a plant that takes two years to complete its growth cycle
Bitter – an herb that stimulates the secretion of digestive juices
Carcinogenic – an herb that can cause cancer
Carminative – an herb that relieves flatulence (gas)
Cleansing – an herb that promotes excretion of waste products
Cooling – an herb that reduces internal "heat" through the excretion of toxins
Deciduous – A term used to refer to trees or shrubs that lose their leaves at the end of the growing season.
Decongestant – an herb that relieves congestion

Demulcent – an herb that soothes irritated tissues
Depressant – an herb that reduces nervous activity
Detoxicant – an herb that removes poisons from the body
Diaphoretic – an herb that promotes sweating and reduces fever
Dioecious – a term used to refer to plants that have male and female parts on separate plants.
Diuretic – an herb that increases urine output
Emetic – an herb that causes vomiting
Emmenagogue – an herb that induces menstruation
Emollient – an herb that soothes and softens the skin
Expectorant – an herb that encourages the expulsion of phlegm
Febrifuge – an herb that reduces fever
Galactogogue – an herb that increases the flow of breast milk
Hepatic – an herb that acts on the liver
Herbaceous – A term used to refer to plants that completely die off each year. No woody stem is left above the ground.
Insecticidal – an herb that kills insects
Laxative – an herb that encourages bowel movements
Mucilaginous – an herb that contains a thick and sticky substance that coats and protects mucous membranes in the body.
Nervine – an herb that supports the functioning of the nervous system
Nutritive – an herb that supports the whole body as a food
Oxytocic – an herb that promotes contractions of the uterus
Perennial – a plant that lives longer than two years
Purgative – an herb that acts as a strong laxative
Relaxant – an herb that relaxes stressed body tissues
Restorative – an herb that restores good health
Rubefacient – an herb that increases blood flow, reddens the skin and promotes the removal of toxins from the body
Sedative – an herb that reduces stress and tension
Sialagogue – an herb that stimulates secretion of saliva
Stimulant – an herb that increases bodily activity
Tonic – an herb that supports the overall functioning of the body and promotes a feeling of well being
Vermifuge – an herb that promotes expulsion of intestinal worms
Vulnerary – an herb that promotes the healing of wounds
Warming – an herb that stimulates circulation and digestion

Tips on How to Make Herbal Teas

Photo by Kamil Porembinski via Flickr/Creative Commons

Making your own herbal teas is probably a lot easier than you might think. The biggest issue is finding the right supplies. I've done all that work for you! The following is an easy step by step guide on how to make the teas, along with a list of good companies to contact for your tea supplies!

The first thing you need to do is get some high quality herbs and tea bags. I have been buying from Monterey Bay Spice Company in San Francisco, CA for many years. They sell herbs in bulk at very reasonable prices as well as boxes of 50 tea bags. Once you have these products, you are ready to make your own teas.

You will notice in my recipes that I refer to the amounts of the herbs needed in "parts". This can mean any measurement, depending on the quantity of tea you want to make. For example, if you want to make just one tea bag and the recipe calls for 1 part Chamomile and ½ part Rose Hips, you can use 1 teaspoon Chamomile and ½ teaspoon Rose Hips. If you want to make enough to last for several weeks, you can use 1 cup Chamomile and ½ cup Rose Hips. It all has to do with how much you would like to make at the time.

Once the herbs have been combined and mixed, put about 1-2 tsp. of the herbal mixture into a tea bag. These bags from Monterey Bay Spice Company are designed to close by the use of heat. At first, I used an iron and that works well, but I found it more convenient to use a flat iron that is normally used on hair. Of course, the flat iron should only be used for sealing the tea bags and not be used interchangeably with your hair styling! I bought one of the cheapest flat irons available, and I store it in my kitchen when not in use. It is much more convenient for me to do this than drag out the iron and ironing board! Hold the tea bag in the flat iron for 5-10 seconds and it should seal. It is a good idea to check for a good seal as I have been surprised on several occasions where the bag didn't seal because I either did not wait long enough for the flat iron to heat up or didn't heat the bag long enough for a good seal.

Once the bag is sealed, you have your herbal tea! Heat up a cup of water, put the tea bag in the cup, let it steep for 3-5 minutes and enjoy! If you like a little sweet flavor in your tea, feel free to add a little honey!

Photo by Michael Lehet via Flickr/Creative Commons

Herbs/Foods Used in the Recipes

Photo by Living in Monrovia via Flickr/Creative Commons

Allspice (*Pimenta dioica*)

Photo by Ryan Snyder via Flickr/Creative Commons

Plant family: Myrtaceae

Also known as: Jamaica pepper, Pimento, Kurundu, Newspice, Myrtle pepper

Native country: Cuba, Central America, Mexico

General information: Allspice is the dried and unripe fruit from the Pimenta dioica plant, and most of this spice comes from Jamaica. In fact, allspice is one of the main spices in jerk seasoning which is popular in Jamaica and the Caribbean. During the flowering season, the trees are grown in "pimento walks" which are very fragrant with the clove-like scent of the herb. The unripe fruit is typically dried in the sun and look like large brown peppercorns when dry. Christopher Columbus discovered allspice in Jamaica although at the time, he thought it was pepper. When he brought the spice back to Spain, it was given the name "pimento" which means "pepper" in Spanish. The name "allspice" was given to this herb in the seventeenth century because of its flavor which is a combination of cloves, cinnamon and nutmeg. Most of the flavor comes from the shell of the berry; therefore, if you are using whole allspice, it is best to grind the entire berry just prior to consumption for the best flavor. The main active volatile oil is eugenol which is weakly antimicrobial.

Growth requirements: Grows best in full sun with well drained and sandy soil.

Plant characteristics: This herb comes from an evergreen tree that grows up to 40 feet and produces small white flowers that bear reddish brown berries.

Oils and other active constituents: Vitamins A, B and C, potassium, manganese, magnesium, iron, selenium, gum, glycosides, tannins, resins, quercetin, sesquiterpenes eugenol, caryophyllene, cineole, phellandrene

Type of herb: Warming, tonic, anesthetic, antiseptic, antimicrobial, antioxidant, carminative

Parts used: Berries, leaves, oil

Internal medicinal uses: Flatulence, indigestion, diarrhea

External medicinal uses: Muscle aches, chest infections, deodorant

Cautions: Avoid use during pregnancy and breast feeding. This herb may interfere with blood clotting medication. Use with caution with the drugs listed below.

Known or possible drug interactions: aspirin, NSAIDS, Coumadin, Warfarin, heparin, Plavix, Fragmin, Orgaran, Normiflo, Lovenox

Catnip (*Nepeta cataria*)

Photo by The County Clerk via Flickr (www.fotopedia.com/items/flickr-2555988821)
Creative Commons Attribution-Share Alike

Plant family: Lamiaceae

Also known as: Catmint, Catswort, Kitty crack, Field Balm, Menta De Gato, Catnep

Native country: Europe, Southwest and Central Asia

General information: It is thought that the active constituent, nepetalactone, is responsible for the dramatic effect that this plant has on cats. The plant stimulates the cat's pheromones resulting in a feeling of euphoria. However, some cats do not respond to this herb, and this lack of response could be genetic. It is reported that only about two thirds of cats will react to this herb. Valerian, another sedative herb, can have similar effects on cats due to the presence of actinidine. This herb has a mild sedative effect on humans and has been used in herbal medicine since the 15th century. In addition, nepetalactone acts as an insect repellant.

Growth requirements: This herb grows on roadsides and mountain regions. It can grow in altitudes up to 5,000 feet and needs sun and moist soil for optimum growth. However, this plant will survive in most soil conditions.

Plant characteristics: Catnip grows up to 3 feet tall. The plant has grayish green leaves and white, pink, blue or lilac flowers with small purple spots.

Oils and other active constituents: Tannins, carvacrol, citronellal, geraniol, nepetol, nepetalactone, thymol, humulene, camphor, nerol, iridoids

Type of herb: Carminative, stimulant to the gastrointestinal system, febrifuge, antibacterial, sedative, strongly antifungal, relaxant

Parts used: Leaves

Internal medicinal uses: Colds, flu, insomnia, flatulence, colic, diarrhea, fever, nervousness

External medicinal uses: Arthritis, hemorrhoids, insect repellant

Cautions: Use with caution during pregnancy. Headache may occur with excessive use.

Known or possible drug interactions: None known

Cayenne Pepper (*Capsicum frutescens*, also *Capsicum minimum*)

Photo by J. Chris Vaughan via Flickr/Creative Commons

Plant family: Solanaceae

Also known as: Chili pepper, Bird pepper, Chili, Red pepper, Aleva pepper, Guinea spice, Cow Horn pepper

General information: This plant was named after the town of Cayenne in French Guinea. Internally, this herb is one of the most powerful circulatory stimulants known to man, and the vitamin C content and antibacterial qualities help to boost the immune system. This herb was first described in 1493 by a physician who was with Christopher Columbus on his voyage to America.

Growth requirements: This plant requires a warm climate and moist soil.

Plant characteristics: Cayenne peppers come from a shrub that grows to 3 feet tall.

Oils and other active constituents: Capsaicin, vitamins A, B6, C and E, riboflavin, potassium, manganese, carotenoids, flavonoids

Type of herb: Stimulant, antibacterial, anti-inflammatory, digestive aid

Parts used: Pods

Internal medicinal uses: Colds, chills, ulcers, nausea, flatulence, hypertension, high cholesterol, boosts metabolism

External medicinal uses: Muscle aches, arthritis, neuralgia, bursitis, psoriasis

Cautions: Excessive consumption may lead to digestive, kidney or liver problems.

Known or possible drug interactions: Aspirin, Warfarin, heparin, Theophylline, Tagamet, Zantac, Pepcid, Nexium, Prilosec, Rolaids, Tums

Chamomile (*Matriacaria recutita*)

Photo by Justin and Elise Snow via Flickr/Creative Commons

Plant family: Asteraceae

Also known as: German chamomile, Camomile

Native country: Europe

General information: This invaluable plant has been used medicinally since the time of the ancient Egyptians who considered it a gift from the sun god, Ra. It was used in love potions during the Middle Ages and was brought to America by the Europeans in the 16th century. Chamomile is the national flower of Russia.

Growth requirements: This plant needs well drained soil and full sun.

Plant characteristics: Chamomile is an annual plant that grows to 2 feet with flowers that are white with yellow centers and look like daisies.

Oils and other active constituents: Chamazulene, chrysin, volatile oils including bisabolol, bitter glycosides, polysaccharides, tannins

Type of herb: Sedative, anti-inflammatory, antispasmodic, antioxidant, antibacterial, antihistamine, analgesic, bitter

Parts used: Flowers

Internal medicinal uses: Insomnia, anxiety, stress, allergies, asthma, psoriasis, hives, atherosclerosis, irritable bowel syndrome, colic, peptic ulcers, motion sickness, premenstrual syndrome, lupus

External medicinal uses: Eczema, abrasions, cuts, burns, mastitis, diaper rash

Cautions: Avoid use during pregnancy. Rarely, atopic dermatitis can result from handling this plant.

Known or possible drug interactions: Warfarin (Coumadin), Cisplatin, Fluorouracil, Methotrexate, Cyclophosphamide, Docetaxel, Paclitaxel, Diazepam, Lorazepam, alcohol, barbituates, narcotics, phenobarbitol, antidepressants

Cinnamon (*Cinnamomum zeylanicum*)

Photo by Fotos Van Robin via Flickr/Creative Commons

Plant family: Lauraceae

Also known as: Ceylon cinnamon, Cassia, Cinnamon twig, Cinnamon bark

Native country: South India and Sri Lanka

General information: This herb has been valued and used since ancient times. In 1536, the Portuguese invaded Ceylon (Sri Lanka) and obtained the much valued cinnamon. Later, in 1770, the Dutch invaded Ceylon, began to cultivate cinnamon and became a dominate supplier of this herb. In 1795, England took over Ceylon. At about this same time, it was discovered that cinnamon could be grown in other areas of the world, so Ceylon no longer had a monopoly over the production of this spice. The aroma and taste of this herb mainly comes from the essential oil cinnamaldehyde.

Growth requirements: This plant needs moist soil and sun to partial shade.

Plant characteristics: This herb comes from an evergreen tree that grows up to 60 feet tall. It has small flowers that are yellowish-white and bears purple berries.

Oils and other active constituents: Mucilage, tannins, resin, gum, sugars, coumarin, calcium oxylate, cinnamaldehyde, eugenol, cinnamate, linalool, beta-caryophyllene, anethole

Type of herb: Astringent, warming, antioxidant, antimicrobial, carminative

Parts used: Dried bark, oil, leaves

Internal medicinal uses: Colds, flu, diarrhea, flatulence and peptic ulcers, menstrual cramps and heavy bleeding, yeast infections, hypertension, arthritis

External medicinal uses: Toothache, halitosis

Cautions: Men with prostate problems should not use cinnamon. People who are allergic to balsam of Tolu should also avoid use of cinnamon oils. Avoid use of this herb if pregnant.

Known or possible drug interactions: None known

Cleavers (*Galium aparine*)

Photo by Joost J. Bakker IJmuiden via Flickr/Creative Commons

Plant family: Rubiaceae

Also known as: Goosegrass, Stickywilly, Stickyweed, Stickyleaf, Clivers, Gripgrass, Hedgeburs, Catchweed, Coachweed, Robin-run-the-hedge

Native country: North and West Asia, Europe

General information: Some species of the Galium family were used to stuff mattresses many years ago and were referred to as "bedstraw". The name "gallium" comes from the Greek word "gala" which means milk. This herb can curdle milk and has been used in cheese making in England for many years. The plant is rich in vitamin C, and a red dye can be extracted from its roots.

Growth requirements: Cleavers is a common weed that grows in moist or grassy regions.

Plant characteristics: This plant is an annual evergreen shrub that grows up to 4 feet with small white or greenish-white flowers and a strong honey odor. The plant bears round, greenish purple fruits. The leaves, stems and fruit are covered with small hooked hairs which cause them to stick to clothing and animal fur.

Oils and other active constituents: Tannins, coumarin, citric acid, flavonoids, asperuloside and other iridoid glucosides, alkanes, polyphenolic acids, chlorophyll, starch, galitannic acid, rubichloric acid, vitamin C

Type of herb: Diuretic, alterative, bitter, cooling, tonic, astringent, laxative, febrifuge, vulnerary, anti-inflammatory, diaphoretic, aperient, antispasmodic

Parts used: Leaves, seeds

Internal medicinal uses: Skin disorders, kidney stones, cystitis, hepatitis, tonsillitis, mononucleosis, measles, chickenpox, hypertension, insomnia, edema, fever

External medicinal uses: Benign breast lumps, psoriasis, eczema, acne, ulcers, swollen lymph nodes, cuts, wounds, sunburn

Cautions: Use with caution during pregnancy.

Known or possible drug interactions: Spironolactone, Triamterene, Loop and Thiazide diuretics

Clove (*Syzygium aromaticum*, also *Eugenia aromaticum*, *Eugenia caryophyllata*)

Photo by epSos.de via Flickr/Creative Commons

Plant family: Myrtaceae

Also known as: n/a

Native country: Indonesia

General information: Since 266 BC, China has used cloves, and this particular spice has become a major part of Chinese cuisine. Cloves were extremely valuable during the Roman times, and Arabs traded this spice profitably during the Middle Ages. When Portugal overtook the Spice Islands and the Indian Ocean trade in the late fifteenth century, they took over the trade of many valuable spices including cloves. Spain briefly took over the trade of cloves followed by the Dutch in the seventeenth century. Eugenol, which comprises up to 90 percent of the volatile oil content of the clove, is responsible for its strong aroma. The word "clove" comes from the Latin word for "nail" as the dried buds resemble nails.

Growth requirements: This spice comes from a tropical evergreen tree that grows near the sea. The tree requires an annual rainfall amount of 60 inches for optimal growth.

Plant characteristics: This evergreen tree grows 30 to 45 feet tall and has pinkish white flowers and purple berries. Cloves are the dried flower buds of the plant.

Oils and other active constituents: Eugenol, vanillin, caryophyllene, tannins, gallotannic acid, crategolic acid, flavonoids, triterpenoids, sesquiterpenes, methyl salicylate

Type of herb: Antiseptic, antibacterial, antifungal, anti-inflammatory, analgesic, warming, stimulant, carminative, anthelmintic, antioxidant, astringent, strongly aromatic

Parts used: Dried buds, oil

Internal medicinal uses: Food poisoning, peptic ulcer, intestinal parasites

External medicinal uses: Toothache, insect bites

Cautions: Children under the age of 6 should not be given clove oil. Medicinal amounts of clove should be avoided by anyone with a history of cancer. This herb may interfere with blood clotting medications due to its high levels of eugenol. Use with caution if taking any of the drugs listed below.

Known or possible drug interactions: Coumadin, Warfarin, heparin, Fragmin, Orgaran, Normiflo, Lovenox, NSAIDS, aspirin

Cramp Bark (*Viburnum opulus*)

Photo by Leonora Enking via Flickr/Creative Commons

Plant family: Caprifoliaceae

Also known as: Guelder rose, Snowball tree, Highbush cranberry, Water elder, European cranberrybush, Cranberry tree, Cranberry bush, Pembina, Pimbina, Whitten tree

Native country: North Africa, Europe, Central Asia

General information: Native Americans made good use of this herb as a diuretic. This plant contains a coumarin called scopoletin that is known to relax the muscles of the uterus and was used in the 19th century to prevent miscarriage. Although some of the common names use "cranberry", this plant is in no way related to the true cranberry.

Growth requirements: This plant requires moist and alkaline soil and sun or partial shade.

Plant characteristics: Cramp bark is a deciduous shrub with small white flowers that produces a bright red fruit.

Oils and other active constituents: Viburnin, valeric acid, tannins, salicosides, resins, coumarins, hydroquinones, scopoletin

Type of herb: Sedative, astringent, bitter, relaxant, antispasmodic

Parts used: Stem bark

Internal medicinal uses: Menstrual cramps, muscle aches, hypertension, irritable bowel syndrome, constipation, colic, asthma, nervousness

External medicinal uses: Aching muscles and cramps

Cautions: Fresh berries are poisonous and may cause stomach upset.

Known or possible drug interactions: None known

Cranberry (*Vaccinium macrocarpon*)

Photo by Andrew Yee via Flickr/Creative Commons

Plant family: Ericaceae

Also known as: Mossberry, Fenberry

Native country: Eastern North America

General information: The name of this plant came from "craneberry". The early American settlers used this term to describe this plant since they felt the look of the plant resembled a crane. The Native Americans used dried cranberries and mixed them with meat and fat to make "pemmican". This was an important dish in their diet during the winter months. Cranberries are related to huckleberries, bilberries and blueberries.

Growth requirements: This plant requires moist, lime-free and sandy soil and sun or partial shade.

Plant characteristics: These deep red fruits come from an evergreen dwarf shrub with dark pink flowers.

Oils and other active constituents: Vitamins A, C and K, manganese, magnesium, calcium, phosphorous, sodium, potassium, fiber, lutein, zeaxanthin, malic acid, tannins, polyphenols, flavonoids

Type of herb: Antibacterial, acidic, antioxidant, possibly anticarcinogenic

Parts used: Fruits

Internal medicinal uses: Kidney stones, incontinence, atherosclerosis, ulcers, gingivitis, urinary tract infection

External medicinal uses: None known.

Cautions: Use with caution if taking any blood thinning medications.

Known or possible drug interactions: Warfarin, Lansoprazole, Omeprazole, aspirin

Cornsilk (*Zea Mays*)

Photo by stereogab via Flickr/Creative Commons

Plant family: Poaceae

Also known as: Maize silk, Indian corn, Zea, Maidis stigma, yu mi shu, Mother's hair, Turkish corn

Native country: Central America

General information: Cornsilk is the female stigma of the corn plant. Its use has been mentioned in Aztec, Mayan and Incan medicine from as far back as 5,000 B.C. It is the most widely cultivated crop in North America, South America and Mexico.

Growth requirements: This plant requires full sun, a temperate climate and moist and well-drained soil.

Plant characteristics: Corn is a grain that grows to 12 feet tall.

Oils and other active constituents: Vitamins A, C and K, rich source of potassium, calcium, fats, gums, resin, sterols, tannin, allantoin, volatile oil, glycosides, saponins, plant acids, alkaloids, hordenine

Type of herb: Diuretic, cooling

Parts used: Stigma, styles, fruits, oils, seeds

Internal medicinal uses: Urinary tract infections, kidney stones, hypertension, PMS, gallstones, cirrhosis, hepatitis, improve blood clotting, enuresis, urethritis, bloating, edema

External medicinal uses: Boils, sores

Cautions: Take with caution if taking medication for blood pressure. Avoid this herb if taking Accupril (quinapril) as side effects have occurred due to high potassium levels.

Known or possible drug interactions: Accupril (quinapril)

Dandelion (*Taraxacum officinale*)

Photo by marcu ioachim via Foto Community/Creative Commons

Plant family: Asteraceae

Also known as: Fairy clock, Pee in the bed, Lion's teeth

Native country: Eurasia

General information: The word "dandelion" comes from the French dent-de-lion which means "lion's tooth". Because of its powerful diuretic effect, this herb has been called "pee in the bed" or in French, "pis en lit". It has been compared to the diuretic drug Furosemide (Lasix), but dandelion can be considered superior to this drug. Furosemide will cause the patient to lose large quantities of potassium, but this does not happen with dandelion because of its high potassium content.

Growth requirements: This plant is considered a weed that requires moist to dry soil.

Plant characteristics: Dandelion grows up to 1 foot and has bright yellow flowers.

Oils and other active constituents: The roots contain vitamins, potassium, asparagines, choline, sugars, pectin, sterols, inulin, glycosides, phenolic acids, taraxacin, triterpenes. The leaves contain vitamins A, B, C, D, and K, potassium, calcium, manganese, iron, zinc and carotenoids. The vitamin A content in this herb is higher than that found in carrots!

Type of herb: Powerful diuretic, blood purifier, cooling, laxative, anti-inflammatory

Parts used: Entire plant

Internal medicinal uses: Constipation, skin disorders, rheumatism, liver disorders, gallbladder disease, digestive aid, anemia, PMS, urinary tract infections, obesity, gout, psoriasis, eczema, acne

External medicinal uses: Snakebite

Cautions: Contact a physician if taking diuretic drugs or medications to control blood sugar levels. Avoid use if taking antibiotics as this herb can alter the concentrations of the drug. Also avoid dandelion if allergic to chamomile or yarrow.

Known or possible drug interactions: Loop and thiazide diuretics, Furosemide Ciprofloxacin (Cipro) and other quinolone antibiotics, Spironolactone, Triamterene, Lithium, antacids

Echinacea (*Echinacea purpurea*, also *Echinacea augustifolia*, *Rudbeckia purpurea*)

Photo by Jordan Meeter via Flickr/Creative Commons

Plant family: Asteraceae

Also known as: Purple coneflower, Black Samson, Missouri Snakeroot, Rudbeckia

Native country: Eastern United States

General information: This drought-tolerant plant was highly valued by the North American Indians and was used commonly for snake bites and wounds. The name comes from the Greek word "echinos" which means "hedgehog".

Growth requirements: This plant prefers sandy soil in full sun and is drought resistant.

Plant characteristics: Echinacea grows up to 20 inches tall. It has purple flowers resembling daisies with orange brown centers and leaves with coarse hairs.

Oils and other active constituents: Essential oils, volatile oils, resins, inulin, betaine, sesquiterpene, glycoside, polysaccharides, polyacetylenes, alkylamides, echinosides, flavonoids, caffeoyl, phenols including cichoric acid and caftaric acid

Type of herb: Blood cleanser, antibacterial, antiviral, anti-inflammatory, alterative, bitter, antioxidant

Parts used: Root, rhizome

Internal medicinal uses: Colds and other viral infections, sore throat, coughs, fever, ear infections, acne and other skin problems, yeast infections, parasitic infections, fungal infections

External medicinal uses: Acne, psoriasis, herpes infections, gargle for sore throats

Cautions: Use of *Echinacea purpurea* over a long period of time can deplete vitamin E. If using this herb over an extended period of time, it would be wise to supplement with vitamin E. Avoid use in children under 1 year of age or if taking immunosuppressant drugs. Use with caution during pregnancy. Possible allergic reactions include rash, asthma, abdominal pain, nausea, dizziness and anaphylaxis. This herb may interfere with anesthesia.

Known or possible drug interactions: Methotrexate, Chemotherapy drugs, Cyclophosphamide, Fluorouracil, Paclitaxel, Econazole, Cisplatin, Docetaxel, immunosuppressants, general anesthesia

Fennel Seed (*Foeniculum vulgare*)

Photo by Rowena via Flickr/Creative Commons

Plant family: Apiaceae

Also known as: Fennel fruit

Native Country: Mediterranean region

General information: The Greeks believed that they could remain slim by eating fennel. This herb has been consumed since the Middle Ages to aid in digestion. Hippocrates and Dioscorides both recommended consuming fennel for the purpose of increasing the flow of breast milk, and the seeds were eaten during Lent to reduce hunger during medieval times. The aniseed flavor of fennel comes from its active constituent anethole. It is one of the main ingredients in absinthe, a popular alcoholic drink in France.

Growth requirements: This plant prefers well drained soil with high lime content and full sun.

Plant characteristics: This perennial herb grows up to 3 feet, has feathery leaves and a stem that resembles celery, and produces small yellow flowers and brown seeds.

Oils and other active constituents: Volatile oils, flavonoids, vitamins, calcium, potassium, oleic acid, linoleic acid, anethole

Type of herb: Antibacterial, antispasmodic, diuretic, has mild estrogenic properties, carminative

Parts used: Seed, roots, leaves, oil

Internal medicinal uses: Indigestion, flatulence, food poisoning, colic, irritable bowel syndrome, motion sickness, dermatitis, coughs, asthma, urinary disorders, glaucoma, hypertension

External medicinal uses: Can be used as a mouthwash for sore throats or gum inflammation

Cautions: Pregnant women and women with reproductive disorders related to estrogen levels should avoid using large quantities of this herb. Consult a physician if you are currently taking the antibiotic Cipro (Ciprofloxacin) as this herb may interfere with the absorption of the antibiotic. People with liver disorders should avoid use of this herb.

Known or possible drug interactions: Ciprofloxacin (Cipro)

Ginger (*Zingiber officinale*)

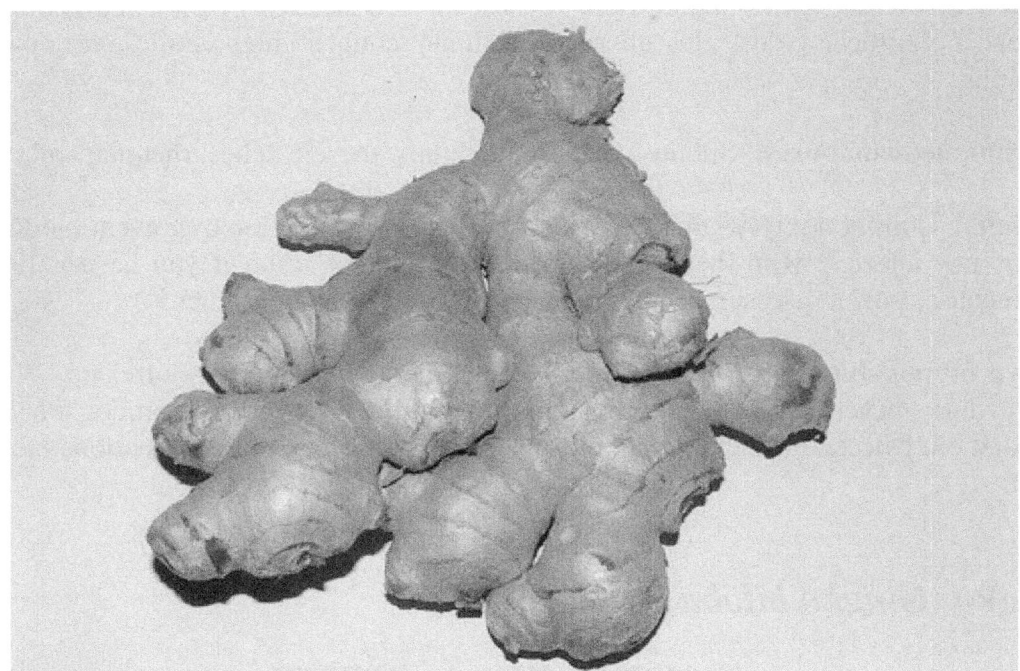
Photo by Delphine Menard via Flickr/Creative Commons

Plant family: Zingiberaceae

Also known as: Jamaica ginger, African ginger, Black ginger

Native country: South Asia

General information: Ginger is a very popular herb and has been used for 2,500 years in Asian medicine. The first recorded use of this herb was during the Han dynasty from 20 to 220 A.D. in China. Ginger is called "vishwabhesaj" in Ayurvedic medicine which means "universal medicine". The flavor of this herb comes from the active constituents gingerols, zingerone and shogaols.

Growth requirements: This plant prefers well drained, moist and tropical soil with full sun to partial shade.

Plant characteristics: This perennial plant grows to 4 feet and bears white or yellowish green flowers.

Oils and other active constituents: Vitamins A and B, minerals, protein, amino acids, starch, fats, volatile oils, oleoresin, zingerone, shogaols, gingerols

Type of herb: Warming, stimulant, expectorant, anti-inflammatory, analgesic, antipyretic, sedative, antibacterial, sialagogue, carminative

Parts used: Rhizome

Internal medicinal uses: Indigestion, nausea, motion sickness, poor circulation, colic, flatulence, diarrhea, colds, flu, allergies, asthma, coughs, high cholesterol, parasitic infections

External medicinal uses: Sprains, menstrual cramps, muscle aches, rheumatism

Cautions: Consult a physician if taking a prescription medication to prevent blood clots. Ginger may interfere with these medications. Use with caution if you have gallstones, inflammatory bowel disease, ulcers or a blockage of the intestinal tract.

Known or possible drug interactions: Chemotherapy drugs, Methotrexate, Warfarin (Coumadin), general anesthesia, heparin, Cisplatin, Cyclophosphamide, Paclitaxel, Fluorouracil, Docetaxel, Ticlopidine, nitrous oxide, blood thinning medications including aspirin

Gingko (*Gingko biloba*)

Photo by Anders Sandberg via Flickr/Creative Commons

Plant family: Gingkoaceae

Also known as: Maidenhair tree

Native country: Central China

General information: The Chinese have been using this herb for almost 5,000 years. Gingko trees can live up to 1,000 years and are highly resistant to fungi, viruses and insects. The tree is often referred to as a living fossil. An example of the hardiness of this tree came after the atomic bomb explosion in Hiroshima, Japan. Six gingko trees survived, recovered from the blast and are healthy and living today! The Gingko tree contains a platelet activating factor (PAF) called ginkgolide that inhibits allergic reactions and is not found in any other plant.

Growth requirements: This tree requires full sun with moist and well drained soil.

Plant characteristics: This deciduous tree can grow up to 115 feet tall. Male trees bear yellow flowers while female trees bear yellowish green fruits that have an unpleasant smell when ripe.

Oils and other active constituents: Flavonoid glycosides, terpenoids including ginkgolide and bilobalides

Type of herb: Antioxidant, stimulant, astringent, antifungal, antibacterial

Parts used: Leaves, oil, seeds

Internal medicinal uses: Memory loss, Alzheimer's disease, dementia, attention deficit disorder, cancer, depression, eye disorders, heart attack, stroke, diabetes, tinnitus, vertigo, asthma, varicose veins, intermittent claudication

External medicinal uses: None known

Cautions: Avoid use if taking MAOIs or SSRIs for depression. A very small number of people have reported nausea, mild headache or orthostatic hypertension after using gingko. Discontinue use if you experience any of these symptoms. Consult a physician if taking any blood thinning medications before using this herb. Avoid use during pregnancy. Known side effects with use include headache, dizziness, restlessness, nausea, vomiting and diarrhea. Avoid use if severely allergic to poison ivy.

Known or possible drug interactions: Aspirin, heparin, Thiazide diuretics, Warfarin (Coumadin), Fluoxetine, Cyclosporine, Paroxetine, Sertraline, Haloperidol, Citalopram, Fluvoxamine, Trazodone, Repaglinide, Glyburide, Glimepiride, Glipizide, Metformin, Ticlopidine

Ginseng (*Panax ginseng*)

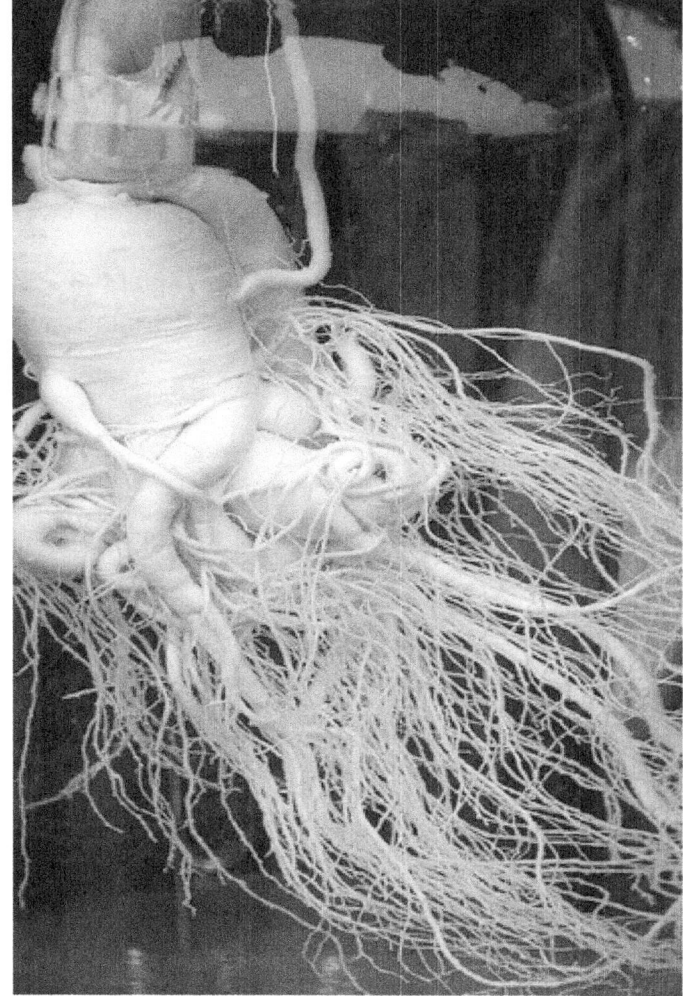

Photo by Chloester via Flickr/Creative Commons

Plant family: Araliaceae

Also known as: Chinese ginseng, Japanese ginseng, Korean ginseng, Ginseng root, Red Ginseng

Native country: China, Siberia, North Korea

General information: "Panax" means "all-heal" in Greek. This herb was discovered over 5,000 years ago has been used in China for over 2,000 years. The word "ginseng" means "man plant". This name was given to the plant because the root branches and sometimes resembles the human body. Its primary active constituents are the ginsenosides, and this amazing herb also contains phytoestrogens.

Growth requirements: This plant requires moist soil and shade for optimum growth.

Plant characteristics: Ginseng grows up to 31 inches tall and takes four years to mature. It has small yellowish green flowers and bears small red berries.

Oils and other active constituents: Vitamins B1, B2 and B12, choline, zinc, copper, magnesium, manganese, calcium, iron, vanadium, saponins, volatile oils, fats, sugars, starch, sterols, pectin, ginsenosides, phytoestrogens

Type of herb: Tonic, stimulant, warming, aphrodisiac, adaptogen, antioxidant, anti-inflammatory

Parts used: Root

Internal medicinal uses: Anxiety, stress, insomnia, impotence, infertility, diabetes, cancer, hypertension, heart attack, shock

External medicinal uses: None known

Cautions: Avoid use during pregnancy and for two weeks prior to surgery. Consult a physician before using ginseng if taking MAOI inhibitors, steroids, Digitalis or Warfarin. Excessive consumption may cause restlessness, headaches and hypertension, nausea, diarrhea and nosebleeds. Use with caution if taking antidepressants.

Known or possible drug interactions: Warfarin (Coumadin), aspirin, NSAIDS, heparin, Normiflo, Lovenox, Fragmin, Orgaran, heart or blood pressure medications, medications used to control blood sugar

Goji Berry (*Lycium barbarum*, also *Lycium chinense*)

Photo by daveeza via Flickr/ Creative Commons

Plant family: Solanaceae

Also known as: Wolfberry, Red medlar, Chinese wolfberry, Murali, Matrimony vine, Mede berry, Duke of Argyll's tea tree, Barbary matrimony vine, Bocksdorn

Native country: Himalayan valleys of China

General information: In the 1730's, the Duke of Argyll brought wolfberries to the United Kingdom. China is currently the top producer of these berries, and they regard the goji as "the longevity fruit". The flavor of the berry is a combination of a strawberry and a raspberry, and they are very high in vitamin C.

Growth requirements: This hardy plant grows in any kind of soil or climate, adapts to poor soil conditions and can survive in drought.

Plant characteristics: The goji plant grows to 3 feet, has lavender flowers, and bears orange-red berries.

Oils and other active constituents: Vitamin A, vitamin B2, vitamin B6 vitamin C, vitamin E, protein, iron, calcium, potassium, zinc, selenium, manganese, copper, alpha-linolenic acid, lutein, zeaxanthin, lycopene, phenols, phytosterols, polysaccharides, antioxidants, amino acids, cystine

Type of herb: Antioxidant, antibacterial, antifungal, anti-inflammatory, adaptogen

Parts used: Berries, leaves

Internal medicinal uses: Possibly useful in the following: cardiovascular disease, vision problems, cancer treatment, digestive disturbances, regulating cholesterol and blood sugar levels, supporting immune system, improving stamina

External medicinal uses: None known

Cautions: Use with caution if you have known pollen allergies.

Known or possible drug interactions: Warfarin (Coumadin), diabetes medications, blood pressure medications

Goldenseal (*Hydrastis canadensis*)

Photo by Keith Robinson via Flickr/Creative Commons

Plant family: Ramunculaceae

Also known as: Yellowroot, Orangeroot, Eye root, Indian turmeric

Native country: North America, Southeast Canada

General information: The North American Indians have used this herb extensively to treat inflammatory conditions involving the mucous membranes. The active constituent, berberine, is responsible for this herb's healing powers. It activates the white blood cells in your body, and these cells attack and kill viruses. A member of the buttercup family, goldenseal was listed as an endangered plant in 1997 and was given international protection. This is a wonderful herb to help boost the effects of other herbs when blended together.

Growth requirements: This plant prefers moist soil and shade for optimal growth.

Plant characteristics: Goldenseal grows to 1 foot and is a spreading plant. It has a thick yellow root and the flower produces a red and inedible fruit similar in appearance to a raspberry.

Oils and other active constituents: Volatile oil, resin, berberine, hydrastine, canadine

Type of herb: Anti-inflammatory, sedative, antibacterial, antiviral, bitter, alterative, decongestant, mild laxative, astringent, antiseptic, anticatarrhal, hepatic, emmenagogue, oxytocic

Parts used: Root, rhizome

Internal medicinal uses: Digestive inflammation, skin infections, periodontal disease, Meniere's disease, pelvic inflammatory disease, painful menstruation, colitis, gastritis, ulcers, liver disorders

External medicinal uses: Gum disease, eczema, conjunctivitis

Cautions: People with high blood pressure and women who are pregnant should avoid using goldenseal. Berberine is known to stimulate the uterus. Avoid use if taking blood thinning medication. Since this herb also destroys beneficial bacteria in the digestive system, limited use is recommended, usually for no more than three months at a time. Use with caution in young children.

Known or possible drug interactions: Warfarin (Coumadin), Tetracycline, Doxycycline, cardiac glycosides protease inhibitors, heparin

Hibiscus (*Hibiscus rosa-sinensis*)

Photo by Tom Raftery via Flickr/Creative Commons

Plant family: Malvaceae

Also known as: Sorrell, Rosemallow, Flor de Jamaica

Native country: Eastern Asia

General information: Since this plant was known to cool the body, Pharaohs in the Nile Valley would drink refreshing hibiscus tea to cool off from the heat. The herb is used in many different hot and cold beverages all around the world with one example being "karkade" which is a popular drink in Egypt. This is a popular plant used in landscaping because of their big and colorful flowers, and tropical hibiscus has been known to survive as long as 50 years. It has a tart flavor similar in taste to cranberry and is very high in Vitamin C.

Growth requirements: This plant prefers warm temperatures, well drained soil and full sun.

Plant characteristics: This annual bush grows anywhere from 12 inches to 40 feet with very showy flowers in many colors.

Oils and other active constituents: Vitamin C, minerals, polysaccharides, glycosides including cyanidin and delphinidin, organic acids including citric, tartaric and maleic acids

Type of herb: Diuretic, laxative, antibacterial

Parts used: Flowers

Internal medicinal uses: Hypertension, high cholesterol, weight loss, upper respiratory tract infections, bloating, constipation, loss of appetite

External medicinal uses: None known

Cautions: Avoid use during pregnancy.

Known or possible drug interactions: Acetaminophen

Hops (*Humulus lupulus*)

Photo by NZ Craft Beer TV via Flickr/Creative Commons

Plant Family: Cannabaceae

Also known as: n/a

Native country: Europe, West Asia, North America

General information: This herb was cultivated as early as the 8th and 9th century but was not widely used until much later. The flowers of the female plant were used to make beer; however, Henry VI and Henry VII banned the use of hops in beer making and referred to the herb an "unwholesome weed". When hops did become more widely used, the Germans named the drink "bier". "Ale" referred to the drink that was made with ground ivy and costmary only. Two types of resins, alpha and beta acids, are present in this plant. Alpha acids have antibiotic activity and contribute to the bitter flavor of beer while beta acids contribute to the bitter aroma of beer. The relaxing effect of this herb may be due to an active constituent called dimethylvinyl carbinol.

Growth requirements: This plant needs sun or partial shade with moist and well drained soil.

Plant characteristics: Hops is an herbaceous and climbing perennial that grows up to 20 feet.

Oils and other active constituents: Fats, amino acids, flavonoid glycosides, volatile oils, bitter resins including alpha and beta acids, tannins, estrogenic compounds, asparagin, dimethylvinyl carbinol

Type of herb: Relaxant, antibacterial, anti-inflammatory, bitter, tonic, diuretic, sedative

Parts used: Female strobiles, leaves, oil

Internal medicinal uses: Insomnia, stress, anxiety, Crohn's disease, irritable bowel syndrome, indigestion

External medicinal uses: Eczema, leg ulcers, herpes, skin infections

Cautions: Those who suffer from depression should avoid use of this herb. The pollen from the plant may cause contact dermatitis. This herb contains a phytoestrogen and should be avoided during pregnancy and by anyone (male or female) with hormone and/or reproductive disorders. Consumption of this plant can be life threatening to dogs.

Known or possible drug interactions: None known

Lavender (*Lavandula augustifolia*, also *Lavandula officinalis*, *Lavandula spica*, *Lavandula vera*)

Photo by Limbo Poet via Flickr/Creative Commons

Plant family: Lamiaceae

Also known as: English lavender

Native country: Mediterranean region

General information: This plant has been used for thousands of years. The Romans used it in baths to add a wonderful aroma, and "lavender pillows" were very popular in the Victorian era. Ancient Greeks referred to the plant as "nardus" or "nard", and it has been mentioned in the Bible in the Song of Solomon.

Growth requirements: This plant can be found in cooler environments in well-drained and sandy soil and full sun.

Plant characteristics: This hardy perennial shrub grows to 24 inches and grows spikes of blue, violet or lilac flowers.

Oils and other active constituents: Camphor, pinene, limonene, linalool, lavendulyl acetate, terpineol, cineole, coumarin, hemiarin, umbelliferone, tannins, flavonoids, triterpenoids

Type of herb: Antibacterial, sedative, relaxant, tonic, antispasmodic, diuretic, digestive aid, antidepressant, anti-inflammatory, carminative

Parts used: Flowers, oil

Internal medicinal uses: Coughs, colds, headache, migraine, anxiety, insomnia, nervousness, irritability, nausea, flatulence

External medicinal uses: Burns, muscle aches, rheumatism, snake bites, insect bites, stings, skin disorders, deodorant

Cautions: Never ingest oil of lavender. Pregnant women should avoid use of oil of lavender. People with gallstones or any disorder of the bile tract should avoid use of this herb.

Known or possible drug interactions: None known.

Lemon Balm (*Melissa officinalis*)

Photo by color line via Flickr/Creative Commons

Plant family: Lamiaceae

Also known as: Balm, Melissa, Sweet Balm, Bee Balm, Cure-All

Native country: Mediterranean region, Western Asia, North Africa

General information: This is a very gentle herb and is safe to use in children. Melissa is the Greek word for honeybee, and this herb was probably named this because it was originally grown to attract bees. It has been cultivated for over 2000 years, and the Arabs used it therapeutically since the 10th century. The flavor of this herb comes from the active constituents geraniol, caryophyllene, citronellal and linalyl acetate. This plant is an excellent insect repellant for mosquitoes.

Growth requirements: This plant prefers sun to partial shade and moist, well drained and sandy soil.

Plant characteristics: Lemon balm is a hardy perennial that grows up to 48 inches tall. The leaves have a distinct lemon scent and are used in herbal medicine. Additionally, the plant bears small white to pale yellow flowers and attracts bees.

Oils and other active constituents: Citronellal, citral, geraniol, eugenol acetate, triterpenoids, rosmarinic acid, polyphenols, flavonoids, tannins, caryophyllene, linalyl acetate

Type of herb: Sedative, antispasmodic, antiviral, antibacterial, cooling, insect repellant, relaxant, antioxidant, carminative

Parts used: Leaves, oil

Internal medicinal uses: Depression, anxiety, nervousness, headache, indigestion, colds, flu, insomnia, digestive aid, flatulence, irritable bowel syndrome, hyperthyroidism

External medicinal uses: Insect repellant, herpes, sores, insect bites, gout

Cautions: Avoid use if you have glaucoma, are taking barbituates or are on thyroid medication.

Known or possible drug interactions: Thyroid hormones, barbituates

Lemon Grass (*Cymbopogon citratus*)

Photo by Clay Irving via Flickr/Creative Commons

Plant family: Cymbopogon

Also known as: Citronella grass, Barbed wire grass, Fever grass, Silky heads, Cha de Dartigalongue, Hierba Luisa, Gavati Chaha

Native country: Sri Lanka and South India

General information: This herb contains very high levels of the essential oils citral and citronellal. The active constituent myrcene may act as a pain reliever. People in the Amazon have used this herb as a tea for sedation, and Brazilians have used it for stomach disorders and nervousness.

Growth requirements: This plant prefers moderate humidity, well-drained soil and full sun.

Plant characteristics: Lemon grass is a tropical and aromatic grass that grows to 5 feet tall.

Oils and other active constituents: Citral, citronellal, myrcene

Type of herb: Bitter, cooling, sedative, antifungal, antibacterial, astringent, antipyretic, analgesic, carminative

Parts used: Oil, leaves, stems

Internal medicinal uses: Feverish illnesses, diarrhea, flatulence, nausea, vomiting, headaches, high cholesterol

External medicinal uses: Arthritis, lice, ringworm, scabies, athlete's foot, sciatica, neuralgia, sprains, tendonitis, insect repellant

Cautions: Use with caution during pregnancy.

Known or possible drug interactions: None known

Lemon Peel (*Citrus limon*)

Photo by Alejandra Owens via Flickr/Creative Commons

Plant family: Rutaceae

Also known as: Lemon

Native country: Possibly Northwest India

General information: Lemons contain 5 to 6 percent citric acid which accounts for their sour taste. This plant first came to Europe in the first century AD and was introduced to America by Christopher Columbus in 1493.

Growth requirements: This plant requires a warm climate but can tolerate poor soil conditions.

Plant characteristics: The lemon tree can grow to 20 feet, has purplish white flowers, and sharp thorns are present on the twigs.

Oils and other active constituents: Vitamins A, B and C, calcium, potassium, bioflavonoids, volatile oils, limonene, mucilage, coumarins, alpha-terpinene, alpha-pinene, citral, pectin, citric acid

Type of herb: Antiseptic, antibacterial, diuretic, astringent, febrifuge, antioxidant

Parts used: Fruit

Internal medicinal uses: Colds, gingivitis, tongue inflammation

External medicinal uses: None known

Cautions: Excessive use may cause erosion of tooth enamel.

Known or possible drug interactions: None known

Licorice Root (*Glycyrrhiza glabra*)

Plant family: Fabaceae

Also known as: n/a

Native country: Mediterranean region, Southwest Asia

General information: This herb has been used in China for over 3,000 years. It was cultivated and processed in Germany since the 11th century. In the late 1550's, the Dominican friars used it in licorice lozenges called pomfrets. Since glycyrrhizin is 50 percent sweeter than sugar, this herb is a great addition to any herbal remedy just for taste. The flavor of licorice comes from its active constituent anethole.

Growth requirements: This plant requires full sun with sandy, well drained and slightly alkaline soil.

Plant characteristics: Licorice is an herbaceous perennial that grows up to 6 feet and is classified as a legume. It is a woody plant that bears clusters of purple, white or pale blue flowers.

Oils and other active constituents: Sugars, starch, sterols, amino acids, gums, wax, glycyrrhizin, asparagines, choline, betaine, flavonoids, isoflavonoids, coumarins triterpenoid saponins, volatile oil, anethole

Type of herb: Anti-inflammatory, laxative, expectorant, antibacterial, antiviral, tonic, antispasmodic, adaptogen

Parts used: Roots and runners of three or four year old plants

Internal medicinal uses: Indigestion, colic, peptic ulcers, irritable bowel syndrome, Crohn's disease, ileitis, leaky gut syndrome sore throats, coughs, bronchitis, asthma, Meniere's disease, cancer, hepatitis, diabetes, allergies, rheumatoid arthritis, lupus

External medicinal uses: Psoriasis, herpes, shingles, eczema

Cautions: Due to the possibility of retention of sodium and potassium, use of this herb is not recommended if you have high blood pressure, are pregnant, have kidney disease, are anemic or are taking any digoxin medication. Avoid this herb if you have a history of hormone-related disorders, hypothyroidism or are using corticosteroids. Excessive consumption may produce edema and hypertension.

Known or possible drug interactions: Corticosteroids, aspirin, ibuprofen, Naproxen, Loop and Thiazide diuretics, Digoxin, Interferon, Risperidone, Etodolac, Isoniazid, Oxaprozin, Nabumetone

Marshmallow (*Althaea officinalis*)

Photo by Phil Sellens via Flickr/Creative Commons

Plant family: Malvaceae

Also known as: Althaea root, Common marshmallow

Native country: Central Russia, West Asia, North Africa, Europe

General information: The use of marshmallow root in herbal medicine originated in Greek medicine. The name althaea comes from the Greek word altha which means "to cure". This herb was widely used in Greek medicine and its use as a healing plant has been recorded as early as the ninth century B.C. The current day marshmallow confectionary does not contain any of the herb.

Growth requirements: This plant grows best in wet and marshy regions and full sun.

Plant characteristics: Marshmallow grows up to 36 inches tall and bears pale pink flowers.

Oils and other active constituents: Mucilage, tannins, asparagin

Type of herb: Expectorant, diuretic, anti-inflammatory, mucilaginous, demulcent, emollient, vulnerary

Parts used: Roots, leaves, flowers

Internal medicinal uses: Peptic ulcers, gastritis, hiatal hernia, cystitis, urethritis, kidney stones, colitis, gastroenteritis, irritable bowel syndrome, constipation, coughs, bronchitis

External medicinal uses: Psoriasis, eczema, boils, abscesses, gingivitis, mastitis, insect bites, gangrene, ulcers, varicose veins

Cautions: Use with caution in diabetics.

Known or possible drug interactions: None known.

Milk Thistle (*Silybum marianum*, also *Carduus benedictus*, *Carduus marianus*)

Photo by Andrew Bossi via Flickr/Creative Commons

Plant family: Asteraceae

Also known as: Blessed thistle, St. Benedict thistle, Holy thistle, Spotted thistle, Mary thistle

Native country: Mediterranean region

General information: This herb has leaves with spots of white on them, and in Europe, these white spots were thought to be from the milk of the Virgin Mary. Milk thistle has been used for over 2000 years to treat disorders of the liver. Silymarin, an active flavolignan in the plant, protects the liver from damage by toxins.

Growth requirements: This plant prefers full sun and slightly alkaline soil.

Plant characteristics: Milk thistle grows up to 5 feet, bears purple and pink flowers (which are edible) and black seeds.

Oils and other active constituents: Mucilage, tannins, cnicine, alkaloids, essential oil, silymarin, linoleic acid, flavonoids

Type of herb: Tonic, diuretic, bitter

Parts used: Roots, seeds, aerial parts

Internal medicinal uses: Digestive disturbances, diabetes, acne, psoriasis, hepatitis, cirrhosis, alcoholism, liver cancer, jaundice, high cholesterol, minimizes the side effects of chemotherapy, increases the flow of breast milk

External medicinal uses: None known

Cautions: May cause vomiting and diarrhea when strong infusions are consumed. This herb may interfere with the effectiveness of birth control pills.

Known or possible drug interactions: Acetaminophen, Chemotherapy drugs, general anesthesia, nitrous oxide, Methotrexate, Haloperidol, Lovastatin, Metronidazole, Paclitaxel, Cisplatin, Pravastatin, Tacrine, Clofibrate

Nettle (*Urtica dioica*, also *Urtica urens*)

Photo by Lauren Tucker via Flickr/Creative Commons

Plant family: Urticaceae

Also known as: Stinging nettle

Native country: Europe, Asia

General information: This herb has one of the highest sources of minerals which makes it very valuable as a tonic. It is very useful in the treatment of gout as it increases the excretion of uric acid. The leaves are covered with small stinging hairs that contain histamine, serotonin and formic acid. These leaves can cause very painful stings.

Growth requirements: This plant prefers sun to partial shade with moist soil that is rich in nitrogen.

Plant characteristics: Nettle is an herbaceous perennial that grows up to 6 feet tall. The leaves are covered with stinging hairs, and the plant produces small green flowers.

Oils and other active constituents: Vitamins A and C, potassium, iron, manganese, silica, sulfur, chlorophyll, histamine, acetylcholine, 5-HTP, formic acid, glucoquinones, serotonin

Type of herb: Tonic, astringent, diuretic

Parts used: Leaves, roots

Internal medicinal uses: Useful in the treatment of anemia, heavy menstrual bleeding, hemorrhoids, eczema, hemorrhage, gout, rheumatoid arthritis, osteoarthritis, hypertension, constipation, nausea, diarrhea, asthma, allergic rhinitis, common cold, kidney disease, urinary tract infection, increases the flow of breast milk, lowers blood sugar levels

External medicinal uses: Nosebleed, hemorrhoids, arthritis, burns, insect bites, gout, sciatica, neuralgia

Cautions: Contact a physician if taking any of the drugs listed below.

Known or possible drug interactions: Diclofenac, Warfarin (Coumadin), Plavix, aspirin, NSAIDS, diuretics, beta blockers, ACE inhibitors, calcium channel blockers

Nutmeg (*Myristica fragrans*)

Photo by Ramesh NG via Flickr/Creative Commons

Plant family: Myristicaceae

Also known as: Jatiphala

Native country: Moluccas and Banda Islands

General information: During the coronation of Emperor Henry VI, nutmeg was one of the spices thrown in the streets of Rome. It has been used since 600 A.D. in Chinese medicine and was believed to get rid of the plague in Elizabethan times. Legend has it that Connecticut was named "The Nutmeg State" because some traders claimed that they could whittle nutmeg out of wood creating a "wooden nutmeg". This term today refers to any kind of fraud. This is the only tropical fruit tree known to yield two separate spices, nutmeg and mace. Nutmeg is the seed produced by the tree while mace is the dry red covering of the seed.

Growth requirements: This plant requires sandy soil and high humidity.

Plant characteristics: Nutmeg is a dioecious evergreen tree that grows up to 40 feet tall with pale yellow flowers.

Oils and other active constituents: Volatile oils eugenol and iso-eugenol, terpenes, terpineol, borneol, oleic and linoleic acids, palmitic acid, lauric acid, myristic acid

Type of herb: Digestive tonic, warming, astringent, bitter, carminative

Parts used: Seed, oil

Internal medicinal uses: Nausea, vomiting, flatulence, colic, indigestion

External medicinal uses: Eczema, rheumatism, toothache

Cautions: This herb should be used sparingly as it is toxic in anything other than small amounts. Ingesting too much nutmeg can cause convulsions, hallucinations and disorientation, severe headache, dizziness and nausea. Avoid use during pregnancy.

Known or possible drug interactions: Diazepam, Ondansetron, Buspirone, Flunitrazepam

Orange Peel (*Citrus sinensis*)

Photo courtesy of Veganbaking.net via Flickr (www.flickr.com/photos/vegan-baking)
Creative Commons Attribution-Share Alike

Plant family: Rutaceae

Also known as: n/a

Native country: Southeast Asia

General information: The orange tree is the most commonly grown fruit tree in the world today. Christopher Columbus introduced the seeds to the Caribbean region in 1493, and Juan Ponce de Leon brought them to Florida in 1513.

Growth requirements: This plant requires a warm climate and a great deal of water.

Plant characteristics: This evergreen tree produces white flowers, and the fruit is a type of berry.

Oils and other active constituents: Citral, d-limonene, vitamins B and C, calcium, magnesium, zinc, iron, potassium, phosphorous

Type of herb: Antioxidant, carminative

Parts used: Fruit, peel

Internal medicinal uses: Appetite stimulant, colds, coughs, flatulence, indigestion, high cholesterol, hypertension

External medicinal uses: Gardeners have been known to use orange peel as a slug repellant.

Cautions: Citral, an active constituent found in orange peel, can interfere with vitamin A synthesis. Be sure to consume plenty of vitamin A rich foods if consuming large amount of orange peel. Excessive consumption of the peel should be avoided in children.

Known or possible drug interactions: Celicard, Fexofenadine, Pravachol, Ivermectin, quinoline antibiotics

Parsley (*Petroselinum crispum*)

Photo by Hlijod.Huskona via Flickr/Creative Commons

Plant family: Apiaceae

Also known as: n/a

Native country: Southeast Europe and Western Asia

General information: This herb was first mentioned in 42 A.D. The active flavonoid apigenin is an antioxidant and reduces allergy symptoms. Parsley is known to freshen breath especially after consuming garlic. The active constituent apiole is a known stimulant to the kidneys.

Growth requirements: This plant prefers sun or partial shade, neutral or alkaline soil and a temperate climate.

Plant characteristics: Parsley is a biennial and herbaceous plant that grows up to 12 inches and produces small yellowish green flowers.

Oils and other active constituents: Vitamins A and C, calcium, iron, phosphorous, manganese, flavonoids, apiole, apiolin, apigenin, myristicin, pinene

Type of herb: Diuretic, bitter, emmenagogue, antioxidant

Parts used: Leaves, seeds, roots, oil

Internal medicinal uses: Urinary tract infections, kidney stones, gout, edema, menstrual disorders, arthritis, anemia

External medicinal uses: When rubbed on the skin, this herb can reduce itching caused by mosquito bites.

Cautions: Do not use this herb during pregnancy.

Known or possible drug interactions: None known

Passionflower (*Passiflora incarnate*)

Photo by Roy Niswanger via Flickr/Creative Commons

Plant family: Passifloraceae

Also known as: Maypops, Wild passionflower, Apricot vine, Blue passionflower

Native country: North, Central and South America

General information: This plant gets its name from the crucifixion of Jesus Christ as follows:
> The three styles represent the three nails used to nail Jesus to the cross
> The five stamens represent the five wounds of Jesus.
> The pointed tips of the leaves represent the lance used to pierce His side.
> The tendrils represent the whips used.
> The ten sepals represent the ten faithful apostles. Peter and Judas were the two that are not included because Peter denied Jesus and Judas betrayed Him.
> The blue and white colors of the flowers represent Heaven and purity.

The Houma tribe of the Native American Indians added this herb to their drinking water and used it as a tonic.

Growth requirements: This plant prefers slightly acidic and sandy soil and full sun.

Plant characteristics: Passionflower is a vine that grows up to 32 feet tall. It bears blue and white flowers and fruit that is shaped like an egg.

Oils and other active constituents: Sugars, gum, sterols, flavonoids, alkaloids, coumarins, phytosterols, maltol, chrysin, organic acids, enzymes, sugars

Type of herb: Relaxant, sedative, bitter, antidepressant, anti-inflammatory, nervine, tonic

Parts used: Flower, vine

Internal medicinal uses: Anxiety, stress, insomnia, irritability, restless legs, hysteria, epilepsy, hypertension, low sex drive, headache, asthma, PMS, shingles

External medicinal uses: Cuts, bruises

Cautions: Avoid use during pregnancy and if you take MAOI inhibitors. Do not give this herb to children under two years of age.

Known or possible drug interactions: MAOI inhibitors

Peppermint (*Mentha piperita*, also *Mentha nigricans*)

Photo by Till Westermayer via Flickr/Creative Commons

Plant family: Lamiaceae

Also known as: n/a

Native country: Great Britain

General information: Peppermint was first reported in 1753 by Corolus Linnaeus. This herb is a hybrid of spearmint and water mint, and the volatile oil menthol is what gives this plant its characteristic taste and smell. The active constituent menthone is a natural pesticide.

Growth requirements: This plant prefers sun to partial shade and moist soil.

Plant characteristics: Peppermint is a hardy and herbaceous perennial that grows up to 3 feet tall. It is a vigorous and invasive plant with purplish pink flowers.

Oils and other active constituents: Menthol, menthone, menthofuran, menthylacetate, rosmarinic acid, azulenes, phytol, flavonoids, carotenoids, tocopherols, choline, tannin, pinene, limonene, pulegone, eucalyptol

Type of herb: Antibacterial, anti-parasitic, antispasmodic, anti-inflammatory, stimulant, decongestant, bitter, anesthetic

Parts used: Leaves, oil

Internal medicinal uses: Colds, indigestion, colic, flatulence, nausea, vomiting, morning sickness, hepatitis, gallstones, headache, irritable bowel syndrome, flu, insomnia

External medicinal uses: Sinusitis, upper respiratory tract infections, rheumatism, neuralgia, ringworm, asthma, headache, insect repellant

Cautions: Avoid prolonged inhalation of the oil of peppermint. Avoid any kind of use in infants.

Known or possible drug interactions: Cisapride (Propulsid)

Rose Hips (*Rosa rugosa, Rosa acicularis, Rosa cinnamomea, Rosa canina*)

Photo by cheekycrows3 via Flickr/Creative Commons

Plant family: Rosaceae

Also known as: Rose haw, Heps, Dog rose

Native country: Europe and West Asia

General information: Rose hips are the fruit of the rose plant that are left behind after the rose has died. They have a tangy flavor similar to cranberries. The tastiest hips come from the Rugusa variety of roses, and they are a very rich source of vitamin C.

Growth requirements: This plant requires well drained soil and five to six hours of full sun.

Plant characteristics: The rose bush is a perennial that grows up to 10 feet tall. The fruit is reddish orange, dark purple or black.

Oils and other active constituents: Vitamins A, B, C, E and K, flavonoids, essential fatty acids, volatile oils, tannins, carotenoids, pectin, plant sterols, anthocyanins, catechins, citric acid, malic acid

Type of herb: Anti-inflammatory, antioxidant, astringent, diuretic, laxative

Parts used: Fruit

Internal medicinal uses: Colds, flu, rheumatoid arthritis, osteoarthritis, diarrhea

External medicinal uses: May reduce the appearance of scars and wrinkles

Cautions: None known

Known or possible drug interactions: None known

Rosemary (*Rosemarinus officinalis*)

Photo by geishaboy500 via Flickr/Creative Commons

Plant family: Lamiaceae

Also known as: n/a

Native country: Mediterranean region

General information: This herb is used in the preparation of the liqueurs, Benedictine and Danziger Goldwasser. Rosmarinus means "dew of the sea" in Latin and refers to the appearance of the pale blue flowers from a distance. Traditionally carried by both mourners at funerals and brides at their wedding, rosemary is a symbol of friendship and loyalty.

Growth requirements: This plant prefers full sun and well drained neutral or alkaline soil.

Plant characteristics: Rosemary is a perennial evergreen shrub that grows up to 3 feet tall. It has very thin green leaves and blue-violet flowers.

Oils and other active constituents: Linalool, verbenol, cineole, borneol, diosmin, rosmanicine, phenolic acids, triterpenic acids

Type of herb: Antibacterial, antifungal, antispasmodic, antioxidant

Parts used: Leaves, oil

Internal medicinal uses: Digestive disturbances, flatulence, indigestion, headaches, poor circulation, rheumatism, cancer, eczema, muscle aches, yeast infection, depression, anxiety

External medicinal uses: Arthritis, neuralgia, dandruff, wounds

Cautions: Do not ingest the undiluted oil. Pregnant women should avoid use of this herb if used medicinally. However, small amounts present in food do not seem to pose a risk.

Known or possible drug interactions: None known

Spearmint *(Mentha spicata*, also *Mentha crispa* or *Mentha viridis)*

Photo by Quinn Dombrowski via Flilckr/Creative Commons

Plant family: Lamiaceae

Also known as: Lamb mint, Garden mint

Native country: Europe and Southwest Asia

General information: Spearmint has been used since Roman times. The pointed tips of the leaves gave rise to the name "spearmint". This herb is popular in mixed drinks such as the mint julep or the mojito.

Growth requirements: This plant prefers sun or partial shade and moist soil.

Plant characteristics: Spearmint is a hardy, herbaceous, creeping and invasive perennial with pink, white or lilac flowers.

Oils and other active constituents: Carvone, limonene, phellandrene

Type of herb: Stimulant, carminative, antifungal, antioxidant

Parts used: Leaves, oil

Internal medicinal uses: Indigestion, flatulence, colic, nausea, vomiting, diarrhea, IBS, gallstones, hirsutism, colds, sore throats, headache

External medicinal uses: Neuralgia, skin inflammation, arthritis, mouth sores

Cautions: Use with caution during pregnancy.

Known or possible drug interactions: None known.

Skullcap (*Scutellaria lateriflora*)

Photo by U.S. Army Environmental Command via Flilckr/Creative Commons

Plant family: Lamiaceae

Also known as: Virginia skullcap, Helmet flower, Mad dogweed, Mad dog skullcap

Native country: North America

General information: This herb was first mentioned during the Han dynasty in China (25-200 A.D.). Skullcap was used by the Cherokee Indians, but people really took note of this herb after an 18th century physician, Dr. Vandesveer, started using it to treat rabies. It then became known as "mad dog skullcap". The active constituent beta-elemene has been shown to have anticarcinogenic properties.

Growth requirements: This plant prefers sun to partial shade and damp soil. It grows well in wetlands.

Plant characteristics: This herbaceous, perennial plant grows up to 18 inches tall and has blue, white or pink flowers.

Oils and other active constituents: Tannin, volatile oil, flavonoid glycosides, bitter principles, diterpenes, beta-elemene

Type of herb: Tonic, nervine, sedative, bitter, antioxidant, analgesic, anticonvulsant, antibacterial, antiviral

Parts used: Leaves

Internal medicinal uses: Depression, headaches, nervousness, insomnia, irritability, neuralgia

External medicinal uses: None known

Cautions: Avoid large doses. Symptoms of overdose include dizziness, erratic pulse, confusion and twitching. Avoid use during pregnancy.

Known or possible drug interactions: Alcohol, barbituates, Dilantin, Depakote, Xanax, Valium, any drug used to treat insomnia

Slippery Elm Bark (*Ulmus rubra* or *Ulmus fulva*)

Photo by Charl de Martigny via Flickr/Creative Commons

Plant family: Ulmaceae

Also known as: Red elm, Sweet elm, Indian elm, Moose elm

Native country: North and Central America

General information: Native American Indians used this herb extensively in the form of decoctions and as a healing salve. The active constituent mucilage coats and soothes the respiratory and digestive mucous membranes. This tree has become scarce due to Dutch Elm disease. In some countries, this herb is under legal restrictions.

Growth requirements: This plant requires full sun and moist soil.

Plant characteristics: Slippery Elm is a deciduous tree bearing reddish brown fruits.

Oils and other active constituents: Tannin, starch, mucilage

Type of herb: Soothing, astringent, mucilaginous, laxative, demulcent

Parts used: Inner bark

Internal medicinal uses: Diarrhea, peptic ulcers, irritable bowel syndrome, indigestion, colitis, diverticulitis, bronchitis, coughs, sore throat

External medicinal uses: Burns, abscesses, wounds, boils

Cautions: Use with caution during pregnancy.

Known or possible drug interactions: None known

Uva Ursi (*Arctostaphylos uva-ursi*)

Photo by Cliff via Flickr/Creative Commons

Plant family: Ericaceae

Also known as: Bearberry, Mountain box, Beargrape, Rockberry, Hogberry, Mountain cranberry, Upland cranberry, Kinnikinnick, Arberry, Crowberry, Foxberry, Hog cranberry, Mountain Tobacco, Sandberry

Native country: Europe, North America

General information: Uva ursi means "bear's grape" in Latin and was named this because bears like to eat the berries from this plant. The first documented use of this herb was in the thirteenth century. Arbutin which is strongly antibacterial is the main active constituent in this herb. The urine needs to be alkaline in order for this herb to be effective against urinary tract infections, so acidic foods should be avoided while taking uva ursi to get the optimum benefit of this herb. "Kinnikinnick" is the name given to uva ursi by the Native Americans when it is mixed with tobacco and smoked.

Growth requirements: This plant prefers sunny but damp conditions and acidic soil.

Oils and other active constituents: Arbutin, volatile oil, resins, flavonoids, tannins, allantoin, phenolic glycosides, essential oils, hydroquinones, tannic acid, ursolic acid, gallic acid

Plant characteristics: Uva ursi is a dwarf evergreen shrub that grows to 6 inches tall. It has trailing stems and white to pink flowers that produce red berries.

Type of herb: Mild diuretic, anesthetic, astringent, antibacterial, sedative

Parts used: Leaves, berries

Internal medicinal uses: Urinary tract infections, prostatitis, kidney disease, heavy menstruation, hemorrhoids, pancreatitis, bloating, arthritis, bronchitis, diabetes

External medicinal uses: Cuts, abrasions

Cautions: Long term use can produce toxic effects. Avoidance of this herb is recommended in those with peptic ulcers and gastroesophageal reflux disease. Pregnant women and children under the age of twelve should avoid use of this herb. Uva ursi should not be used as a replacement for medical treatment of a urinary tract infection.

Known or possible drug interactions: Loop and Thiazide diuretics, Ephedrine, Pseudoephedrine, Atropine, Lomotil, Lonox, Spironolactone, Triamterene, Cardec DM, Coedine, Theophylline, Aminophylline

Wild Yam (*Dioscorea villosa*)

Photo by Dave Bonta via Flickr/Creative Commons

Plant family: *Dioscoreaceae*

Also known as: Colic root, Rheumatism root

Native country: North America

General information: Russell E. Marker, an organic chemist, discovered that he could produce progesterone from wild yam in 1943. Diosgenin, a phytoestrogen found in wild yam, was the only hormonal source used to make the contraceptive pill until 1970.

Growth requirements: This plant prefers sun to partial shade and well-drained soil. It grows well in damp thickets and woodlands.

Plant characteristics: Wild yam is a twining and tuberous vine that grows to 15 feet and has small yellowish green or greenish white flowers.

Oils and other active constituents: Steroidal saponins, tannins, alkaloids, phytosterols, starch, diosgenin

Type of herb: Antispasmodic, anti-inflammatory, diuretic, carminative

Parts used: Root, rhizome

Internal medicinal uses: Menstrual cramps, threatened miscarriage, labor pain, flatulence, colic, irritable bowel syndrome, diverticulitis, Crohn's disease, rheumatoid arthritis, neuralgia

External medicinal uses: Used as a cream for menopausal symptoms

Cautions: Avoid use in small children. Contact your physician before use if on hormone replacement therapy or birth control pills.

Known or possible drug interactions: None known

Maria's Mixes Herbal Tea Recipes

Photo by grendelkhan via Flickr/Creative Commons

About Maria's Mixes, LLC

Maria's Mixes, LLC came about as a result of experimenting with herbs after I received my Master's degree in Holistic Nutrition and Family Herbalist Certificate from Clayton College of Natural Health. With the knowledge that I gained from my coursework, I developed a tonic tea to help support overall health. It turned out to be quite good and soon, many people were asking me to make some for them! I developed a couple more blends, but I drank them myself or gave them to friends and family. In 2009, a co-worker tried one of my teas. She was so excited about it and told me I should go into business. I thought about it for a while, but with a little extra coaxing from her and another employee, I decided to give it a shot.

The first tea that I released when I opened the business was Cleavers and Wild Nettle. This was the very first tonic tea that I developed and it was in high demand! I continued to develop different blends, and with each one, I would try to target a specific body system or an individual disease or disorder. Through a mutual friend, I developed Brady's Blend, a tea specifically developed for a non profit organization called Brady's Smile, Inc. This wonderful organization helps families who have critically ill children who are in the hospital. For more information on this organization, see the Brady's Blend tea recipe below. As the business grew, I was asked to develop blends for a wedding, a baby shower, and even my godson's preschool!

However, in 2010, I decided to close the business. Many factors played into this decision. Insurance costs and lack of sufficient time to make this a profitable business were two of the main deciding factors. I still make tea for close family and friends, but I do miss the business. Then, I came up with this great idea to write a book and share the recipes, and this is where I am today…..I hope you enjoy them!

Cleavers and Wild Nettle

Photo of cleavers on log by Holy Outlaw via Flickr/Creative Commons

This tea blend was developed to help support general health. Cleavers and nettle are both tonic herbs, and nettle has a very high vitamin and mineral content. All three herbs are diuretic with dandelion being the strongest. Dandelion and cleavers also have laxative effects. These diuretic and laxative effects are helpful in the elimination of toxins in the body.

To make the tea, combine the following:

1 Part Dandelion
1 Part Cleavers
1 Part Nettle
1 Part Licorice Root
1 Part Crystallized ginger, minced

Mix the herbs well and place in either a diffuser or a tea bag (see "Tips on How to Make Herbal Teas" on page 15). Heat up a cup of water, let the diffuser or tea bag steep for 2 to 5 minutes and enjoy! This blend already has some sugar in it from the crystallized ginger, so further sweetening may not be necessary.

Ginger, Fennel and Peppermint

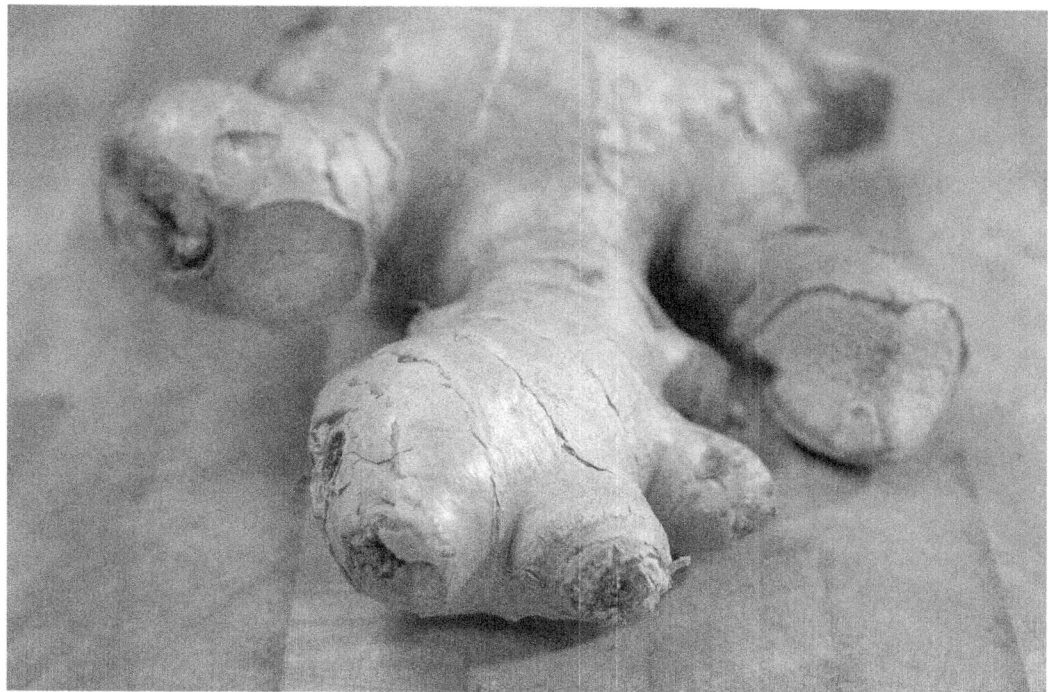
Photo of ginger root by heymrleej via Fotopedia/Creative Commons

This top selling blend was developed for those suffering from mild nausea or recovering from food poisoning or other gastrointestinal illness. But, many people who have tried this tea love it and drink it just for the flavor! As stated before, this tea will not cure any illness, but it may aid in settling an upset stomach. All of the herbs in this blend are soothing to the digestive tract. Ginger and peppermint are well known herbs useful in the treatment of nausea. In addition, peppermint is also anti-inflammatory and antibacterial. Fennel is known to be an excellent digestive aid, and cramp bark relieves any muscle spasms. Marshmallow and slippery elm are added for their mucilage content which is soothing to the digestive tract.

1 Part Crystallized Ginger, minced
1 Part Fennel Seed
1 Part Peppermint
1 Part Cramp Bark
1 Part Marshmallow
1 Part Slippery Elm

Mix all the herbs well and put into a diffuser or tea bag (see "Tips on How to Make Herbal Teas" on page 15). Heat up a cup of water and allow the tea to steep for 2 to 5 minutes. Remove the diffuser or tea bag and enjoy!

Rose Hips and Orange Peel

Photo of rose hips by Leonora Enking via Flickr/Creative Commons

This blend was developed to support the immune system during cold and flu season. In developing this tea blend, I wanted to include herbs that were particularly high in vitamin C and were known to help support the body during times of infection. Rose hips have a very high concentration of vitamin C as does orange peel. Lemon grass, peppermint and goldenseal have antibacterial properties which would be very helpful during times of infection. Additionally, peppermint and goldenseal have anti-inflammatory properties, and chamomile, lemon grass and goldenseal were added for their relaxing and sedative properties. Slippery elm has a high mucilage content which has a soothing effect on the digestive system.

2 Parts Rose Hips
2 Parts Orange Peel
2 Parts Lemon Grass
2 Parts Peppermint
1 Part Chamomile
1 Part Slippery Elm
1 Part Goldenseal

Mix all herbs well and place about a tablespoon in a diffuser or tea bag (see "Tips on How to Make Herbal Teas" on page 15). Heat up a cup of water, allow the diffuser or tea bag to steep for 2 to 5 minutes, remove diffuser or tea bag and enjoy! The peppermint, lemon grass and orange peel gives this blend a great flavor, but if you like it sweeter, you can add a spoonful of honey to this tea!

Chamomile, Hops and Catnip

Photo of hops by David Blaikie via Flilckr/Creative Commons

This highly relaxing tea blend is helpful for those who would like to get a good night of sleep! The herbs used in this blend are well known as sedatives and are great to use to relax after a long day or if you suffer from insomnia. Chamomile, hops, catnip and passionflower are all known to have relaxing and sedative effects. Passionflower has been found useful in the treatment of restless leg syndrome and may help those who have trouble sleeping due to this condition. Marshmallow has been added for its soothing properties. Cinnamon and nutmeg were included for flavor, but these herbs also have their own health benefits.

2 Parts Chamomile
2 Parts Hops
1 Part Catnip
1 Part Passionflower
1 Part Marshmallow
½ Part Cinnamon
¼ Part Nutmeg

Mix all of the herbs well and put a tablespoon or so in a diffuser or tea bag (see "Tips on How to Make Herbal Teas" on page 15). Heat a cup of water, let the diffuser or tea bag steep about 2 minutes, remove the diffuser/tea bag and enjoy! If you would like a sweeter flavor, just add a spoonful of honey.

The Perfect Blend

Photo of passion flower by Just started to learn/reCreation via Flickr/Creative Commons

A good friend of mine was getting married, and she asked me to supply small containers of tea to be used as wedding favors. She wanted her very own tea blend, and she asked for it to be named "The Perfect Blend". I had so much fun working on this project! We ended up with small metal tins, each containing 4 tea bags. We put little mauve colored ribbons on each tin, and they looked so nice sitting on the tables during the wedding reception!

I basically wanted to come up with a "love blend" that was not only nutritious but also gave a little "boost" of energy. The ginseng and cayenne pepper were added for this purpose. Nettle and licorice are tonics and full of nutrients while the marshmallow was added for the soothing properties. Cinnamon and ginger give this blend its flavor while adding additional health benefits.

2 Parts Passionflower
2 Parts Ginseng
2 Parts Cinnamon
1 Part Nettle
1 Part Licorice
1 Part Marshmallow
1 Part Crystallized Ginger
Dash Cayenne Pepper

Mix all of the herbs well and put about a teaspoonful of the mixture into a tea bag or diffuser (see "Tips on How to Make Herbal Teas" on page 15). Heat up a cup of water, allow the tea bag or diffuser to steep for 2 to 5 minutes, remove and enjoy. This blend has a very sweet taste to it due to the cinnamon and crystallized ginger, so further sweetening may not be necessary.

Lemon Balm and Chamomile

Photo of lemon balm by color line via Flickr/Creative Commons

I wanted to develop a mild tea that would be safe for everyone to use, including children. The following blend is a relaxing combination of some very safe herbs. It is useful to drink this tea at night after a long day or if you suffer from insomnia.

1 Part Lemon Balm
1 Part Chamomile
1 Part Marshmallow
1 Part Orange Peel

Mix the herbs together and place about a teaspoonful into a diffuser or tea bag (see "Tips on How to Make Herbal Teas" on page 15). Heat up a cup of water, let the diffuser or tea bag steep for 2 to 5 minutes, remove and enjoy. Add a little honey if you like a sweeter taste.

Brady's Blend

Photo of lavender by Jack Wolf via Flickr/Creative Commons

I was blessed to be introduced to Annie Hinton, founder of Brady's Smile, Inc. This wonderful organization helps families in the northeast U.S. whose children are sick and in the hospital. Through a mutual friend, Annie and I came to know each other, and I decided to supply her organization with some of my tea. I developed a blend that would help to relax the parents of these sick children while giving nourishment to the nervous system. This blend came to be known as "Brady's Blend". Skullcap is a wonderful nervine while lavender, chamomile and lemon balm are all good relaxant herbs. Goji berries are loaded with nutrients and are a great food to include for anyone under significant stress. For more information on Brady's Smile, Inc. including other ways to support this incredible organization, please visit www.bradyssmile.org.

1 Part Lavender
1 Part Chamomile
1 Part Skullcap
1 Part Lemon Balm
Goji Berry, minced

Mix all of the herbs together and place about a tablespoonful into a tea bag or diffuser (see "Tips on How to Make Herbal Teas" on page 15). Heat up a cup of water and let the tea bag or diffuser steep for 2 to 5 minutes. Remove and enjoy! Add a little honey if you like a sweeter taste.

Milk Thistle and Allspice

Photo of milk thistle by Andrew Bossi via Flickr/Creative Commons

Many people asked me about developing a tea blend that would help to detoxify the body. I came up with the following blend that utilizes several herbs useful in the detoxification process. Milk thistle is a powerful liver detoxifier, while dandelion is a powerful diuretic. Both herbs are great to add to any detoxification blend. Wild yam was added for its diuretic and anti-inflammatory effects. Rosemary, clove and allspice were included not only for the flavor but for their nutritive qualities.

2 Parts Milk Thistle
½ Part Allspice
3 Parts Dandelion
3 Parts Wild Yam
1 Part Rosemary
1 Clove per tea bag

Mix all of the herbs together and place about a tablespoon of the mixture into a tea bag or diffuser (see "Tips on How to Make Herbal Teas" on page 15). Heat up a cup of water, place the diffuser or tea bag into the cup and let steep for 2 to 5 minutes. Remove and enjoy. A little bit of honey will help to sweeten this blend.

Cranberry and Allspice Autumn Blend

Photo of cranberries by Rene Schwietzke via Fllickr/Creative Commons

In my desire to come up with a blend that would be delicious in the fall, I decided to also create a tea that would support the urinary tract. Uva ursi, cornsilk, parsley and cranberries are all diuretics and work on the urinary tract to help support its function. Marshmallow is added for its soothing properties due to the high mucilage properties, and allspice is added for taste and nutritive benefits.

Note: This blend should not be used as a treatment for a urinary tract infection. If signs of an infection are present, a physician should always be consulted.

1 Part Marshmallow
1 Part Uva Ursi
1 Part Cornsilk
¼ Part Parsley
¼ Part Allspice
Several minced cranberries per tea bag

Mix all of the herbs and cranberries together and place about a tablespoon in a diffuser or tea bag (see "Tips on How to Make Herbal Teas" on page 15). Heat up a cup of water, place the diffuser or tea bag in the cup and let steep for 2 to 5 minutes. Remove and enjoy! A little bit of honey will help to sweeten this blend.

Santa's Christmas Mint Tea

Photo of spearmint by Quinn Dombrowski via Flilckr/Creative Commons

When I think of herbs and Christmas, the first thing that comes to my mind is peppermint! I developed this "Christmas tea" with mint as the main flavor and other herbs that help to support the immune system. What could be better than enjoying a nice cup of mint tea on a cold winter's night?

Echinacea and goldenseal together will strongly help support the immune system. These two herbs work exceptionally well together. Peppermint and spearmint are included for taste, but these two herbs also have plenty of benefits of their own!

1 Part Peppermint
1 Part Spearmint
1 Part Echinacea
½ Part Goldenseal

Mix all of the herbs together and place about a tablespoon of the mixture in a diffuser or tea bag (see "Tips on How to Make Herbal Teas" on page 15). Heat up a cup of hot water, place the diffuser or tea bag into the cup and let steep for 2 to 5 minutes. Remove and enjoy! The mint taste of this tea is so good that in my opinion, it doesn't need any added sweetener.

Jefferson Tea

Photo of hibiscus by umjanedoan via Flickr/Creative Commons

My dear godson, Heath, attended a wonderful pre-school in the Chicago area. As part of their fundraising, I developed a tea blend for the school and donated several tins of this tea to their event. This tea is named after the school, and it was an absolute pleasure to work with them! I thought about mothers of school children in my development of this tea, and the herbs included improve energy levels and reduce stress.

Ginseng is a well known adaptogen and helps to reduce stress. Skullcap also helps with stress levels through its nervine activity. Orange peel, lemon balm and hibiscus are all added for flavor, although these herbs have many nutritive qualities. Lemon balm is also a well known relaxant.

2 Parts Orange Peel
2 Parts Lemon Balm
1 Part Skullcap
1 Part Hibiscus
¼ Part Ginseng

Mix all of the herbs together and add about a tablespoon of the mixture to a tea bag or diffuser (see "Tips on How to Make Herbal Teas" on page 15). Heat up a cup of water, place the diffuser or tea bag in the cup and let steep for 2 to 5 minutes. Remove and enjoy! This probably won't need any additional honey because the hibiscus gives the tea a wonderful flavor!

Lullaby Lemon

Photo of lemon by Lori Grieg via Flickr/Creative Commons

A friend of mine asked me to develop a tea for an upcoming baby shower. She came up with the name of the tea which I think is just adorable! We definitely wanted a lemon flavor to this tea, so I included lemon balm, lemon peel and lemon grass. Catnip and chamomile were added for their relaxing and sedative effects, and hibiscus was added for both color and flavor.

2 Parts Hibiscus
2 Parts Catnip
1 Part Chamomile
1 Part Lemon Balm
1 Part Lemon Peel
1 Part Lemon Grass

Mix all of the herbs together and put about a tablespoon of the mixture in a diffuser or tea bag (see "Tips on How to Make Herbal Teas" on page 15). Heat up a cup of water, place the diffuser or tea bag in the cup and let steep for 2 to 5 minutes. Remove and enjoy! The hibiscus adds a wonderful flavor and color to this blend, so additional sweetening is probably not needed.

Passionflower and Chamomile

Photo of chamomile byFlare via Flickr/Creative Commons

I developed this blend for someone who was suffering from dementia, arthritis, stress and other medical problems associated with aging. The gingko was included for its memory enhancing properties, and the passion flower and chamomile were added for their relaxing benefits. Crystallized ginger helps with any stomach upset, and hibiscus adds a wonderful flavor and color to the blend.

1 Part Passionflower
1 Part Chamomile
1 Part Gingko
1 Part Hibiscus
1 Part Crystallized Ginger

Mix all of the herbs together and place about a tablespoon of the mixture into a diffuser or tea bag (see "Tips on How to Make Herbal Teas" on page 15). Heat up a cup of water, place the tea bag or diffuser into the cup and allow to steep for 2 to 5 minutes. Remove and enjoy! Because of the flavor of the hibiscus and the sweetness of the crystallized ginger, addition of honey to this blend is not necessary.

Echinacea and Cinnamon

Photo of Echinacea by Randy OHC via Flickr/Creative Commons

This tasty blend is great to drink when recovering from a cold or the flu. Echinacea helps to boost the immune system, and peppermint and ginger are great at calming an upset stomach. Cinnamon was added to this blend for flavor, but it also has its own health benefits!

1 Part Echinacea
1 Part Cinnamon
1 Part Peppermint
1 Part Crystallized Ginger

Mix all of the herbs together and place about a tablespoon of the mixture into a diffuser or tea bag (see "Tips on How to Make Herbal Teas" on page 15). Heat up a cup of water, place the diffuser or tea bag into the cup and let steep for 2 to 5 minutes. Remove and enjoy! Additional sweetening of this blend may not be necessary due to the crystallized ginger.

Refreshing Mint Sun Tea

Photo of peppermint tea by Rupert Ganzer via Flickr/Creative Commons

I wanted to develop a nice and refreshing iced tea to serve on hot, sunny, summer days. Mint flavor is always refreshing, so I included peppermint and spearmint for the main flavor of the tea. Passion flower was added for its relaxant properties while gingko was included for its adaptogenic properties. I finished the blend off with goldenseal as it is a great tonic herb.

1 Part Goldenseal
1 Part Gingko
1 Part Passionflower
1 Part Spearmint
1 Part Peppermint

Mix all of the herbs together and place into a large tea container. Fill the container with water and let the mixture steep all day in full sun. Strain off the herbs and refrigerate the tea for several hours. Serve over ice.

Recommended Companies for Herbal Tea Supplies

Photo of rosemary by Chris Gladis via Flickr/Creative Commons

Dried herbs, tea bags, diffusers

Monterey Bay Spice Company
719 Swift Street
Suite 62
Santa Cruz, CA 95060
1-800-500-6148
support@herbco.com
www.herbco.com

Dried berries (cranberries, goji berries)

Nuts.com
http://nuts.com
1-800-558-6887

Tea pots, cups, other tea supplies

Teavana
3630 Peachtree Road, NE
Atlanta, GA 30326
www.teavana.com
Log on to their site to find a location near you.

Quick Herb-Drug Interaction Guide

Accupril - Cornsilk
ACE inhibitors - Nettle
Acetaminophen – Hibiscus, Milk Thistle
Alcohol – Chamomile, Skullcap
Aminophylline – Uva ursi
Antacids - Dandelion
Antidepressants - Chamomile
Aspirin – Allspice, Cayenne pepper, Clove, Cranberry, Ginger, Gingko, Ginseng, Licorice, Nettle
Atropine – Uva ursi
Barbituates – Chamomile, Skullcap
Beta blockers - Nettle
Buspirone - Nutmeg
Calcium channel blockers - Nettle
Cardec DM – Uva ursi
Cardiac glycosides - Goldenseal
Celicard – Orange peel
Chemotherapy drugs – Echinacea, Ginger, Milk thistle
Ciprofloxacin – Dandelion, Fennel
Cisapride - Peppermint
Cisplatin – Chamomile, Echinacea, Ginger, Milk thistle
Citalopram - Gingko
Clofibrate – Milk thistle
Coedine – Uva ursi
Corticosteroids - Licorice
Cyclophosphamide – Chamomile, Echinacea, Ginger
Cyclosporine - Gingko
Depakote - Skullcap
Diazepam – Chamomile, Nutmeg
Diclofenac - Nettle
Digoxin - Licorice
Dilantin - Skullcap
Docetaxel – Chamomile, Echinacea, Ginger
Doxycycline - Goldenseal
Econazole - Echinacea
Ephedrine – Uva ursi
Etodolac - Licorice
Fexofenadine – Orange peel
Flunitrazepam – Nutmeg

Fluorouracil – Chamomile, Echinacea, Ginger
Fluoxetine – Gingko
Fluvoxamine - Gingko
Fragmin – Allspice, Clove, Ginseng
General anesthesia – Ginger, Milk thistle
Glimepiride - Gingko
Glipizide - Gingko
Glyburide - Gingko
Haloperidol – Gingko, Milk thistle
Heparin – Allspice, Cayenne pepper, Clove, Ginger, Gingko, Ginseng, Goldenseal
Ibuprofen - Licorice
Immunosuppressants - Echinacea
Interferon - Licorice
Isoniazid - Licorice
Ivermectin – Orange peel
Lansoprazole - Cranberry
Lithium - Dandelion
Lomotil – Uva ursi
Lonox – Uva ursi
Loop diuretics – Cleavers, Dandelion, Licorice, Nettle, Uva ursi
Lorazepam - Chamomile
Lovastatin – Milk thistle
Lovenox – Allspice, Clove, Ginseng
MAOI inhibitors – Passion flower
Metformin - Gingko
Methotrexate – Chamomile, Echinacea, Ginger, Milk thistle
Metronidazole – Milk thistle
Nabumetone - Licorice
Naproxen - Licorice
Narcotics - Chamomile
Nexium – Cayenne pepper
Nitrous oxide – Ginger, Milk thistle
Normiflo – Allspice, Clove, Ginseng
NSAIDS – Allspice, Clove, Ginseng, Nettle
Omeprazole - Cranberry
Ondansetron - Nutmeg
Orgaran – Allspice, Clove, Ginseng
Oxaprozin - Licorice
Paclitaxel – Chamomile, Echinacea, Ginger, Milk thistle
Paroxetine - Gingko
Pepcid – Cayenne pepper
Phenobarbitol - Chamomile
Plavix – Allspice, Nettle
Pravachol – Orange peel

Pravastatin – Milk thistle
Prilosec – Cayenne pepper
Propulsid - Peppermint
Protease inhibitors - Goldenseal
Pseudoephedrine – Uva ursi
Quinoline antibiotics – Dandelion, Orange peel
Repaglinide - Gingko
Risperidone - Licorice
Rolaids – Cayenne pepper
Sertraline - Gingko
Spironolactone – Cleavers, Dandelion, Uva ursi
Tacrine – Milk thistle
Tagamet – Cayenne pepper
Tetracycline - Goldenseal
Theophylline – Cayenne pepper, Uva ursi
Thiazide diuretics – Cleavers, Dandelion, Gingko, Licorice, Nettle, Uva ursi
Thyroid hormones – Lemon balm
Ticlopidine – Ginger, Gingko
Trazodone - Gingko
Triamterene – Cleavers, Dandelion, Uva ursi
Tums – Cayenne pepper
Valium - Skullcap
Warfarin (Coumadin) – Allspice, Cayenne pepper, Chamomile, Clove, Cranberry, Ginger, Gingko, Ginseng, Goji berry, Goldenseal, Nettle
Xanax - Skullcap
Zantac – Cayenne pepper

Quick Herb vs. Diseases/Disorder Charts

About the Charts

The following charts were developed as a quick reference guide to show which herbs may be useful in a particular disease or disorder. Since this book is about herbal teas, I have included only the herbs that may be helpful if used internally. The external uses can be found under the description of the individual herb found earlier in this book but are not included here.

The charts have been divided into diseases and disorders of each individual body system. Each chart has a list of the conditions affecting the system and which herbs may be beneficial in each condition. By using these charts, you will be able to see which tea or teas in this book may give you the most benefit. Additionally, if you want to add herbal products to your regime in another manner, these charts may give you a clearer picture of which herbs to include in your diet.

As I have stated before, these herbs should not be viewed as a cure for any condition. These herbs should be used as an adjunct to other medical treatment only after physician consultation to insure there will be no interactions with medications.

CARDIOVASCULAR DISEASES/DISORDERS

	Atherosclerosis	Cardiovascular disease	Heart attack	High blood pressure	High cholesterol	Intermittent claudication	Poor circulation	Stroke						
Cayenne				✓	✓									
Chamomile	✓													
Cinnamon				✓										
Cleavers				✓										
Cornsilk				✓										
Cramp bark				✓										
Cranberry	✓													
Fennel				✓										
Ginger					✓		✓							
Gingko		✓				✓	✓							
Ginseng		✓		✓										
Goji Berry	✓				✓									
Hibiscus				✓	✓									
Lemon Grass					✓									
Milk Thistle					✓									
Nettle				✓										
Orange Peel				✓	✓									
Passion Flower				✓										
Rosemary							✓							

DIGESTIVE DISEASES/DISORDERS

	Colic	Colitis	Constipation	Crohn's disease	Diarrhea	Diverticulitis	Flatulence	Food poisoning	Gastritis	Gastroenteritis	Hiatal hernia	Ileitis	Indigestion	Intestinal parasites
Allspice					✓		✓							
Catnip	✓				✓		✓							
Cayenne							✓							
Chamomile	✓													
Cinnamon					✓		✓							
Clove								✓						✓
Cramp Bark	✓		✓											
Dandelion			✓											
Fennel	✓						✓	✓					✓	
Ginger	✓				✓		✓						✓	
Goldenseal		✓							✓					
Hibiscus			✓											
Hops				✓									✓	
Lavender							✓							
Lemon Balm							✓						✓	
Lemon Grass					✓		✓							
Lemon Peel							✓							
Licorice	✓			✓									✓	✓
Marshmallow		✓	✓						✓	✓	✓			
Nettle			✓		✓									
Nutmeg	✓						✓						✓	
Orange Peel							✓						✓	
Peppermint	✓						✓						✓	
Rose Hips					✓									
Rosemary							✓						✓	
Spearmint	✓				✓		✓						✓	
Slippery elm		✓			✓	✓							✓	
Uva Ursi														
Wild Yam	✓			✓			✓							

DIGESTIVE DISEASES/DISORDERS (CONT.)

	Irritable bowel syndrome	Leaky gut syndrome	Loss of appetite	Nausea	Peptic ulcer	Vomiting
Cayenne				✓		
Chamomile	✓				✓	
Cinnamon					✓	
Clove					✓	
Cramp Bark	✓					
Fennel	✓					
Ginger				✓		
Hibiscus			✓			
Hops	✓					
Lavender				✓		
Lemon Balm	✓					
Lemon Grass				✓	✓	
Licorice	✓	✓			✓	
Marshmallow	✓				✓	
Nettle				✓		
Nutmeg				✓	✓	
Peppermint	✓			✓	✓	
Spearmint	✓			✓	✓	
Slippery elm	✓				✓	
Wild Yam	✓					

EYE/EAR/MOUTH DISEASES/DISORDERS

	Conjunctivitis	Eye disorders	Gingivitis	Glaucoma	Meniere's disease	Motion sickness	Tinnitus	Tongue inflammation	Vertigo			
Chamomile						✓						
Cranberry			✓									
Fennel				✓		✓						
Ginger						✓						
Gingko		✓					✓					
Goji Berry		✓										
Goldenseal	✓				✓							
Lemon Peel			✓					✓				
Licorice					✓							

GALLBLADDER/LIVER/PANCREAS DISEASES/DISORDERS

	Abnormal blood sugar	Alcoholism	Cirrhosis	Diabetes	Gallbladder disease	Gallstones	Hepatitis	Jaundice	Liver cancer	Liver disease	Pancreatitis
Cleavers							✓				
Corn Silk			✓			✓	✓				
Dandelion					✓					✓	
Gingko				✓							
Ginseng				✓							
Goji Berry	✓										
Goldenseal										✓	
Licorice				✓		✓					
Milk Thistle		✓	✓	✓			✓	✓	✓	✓	
Peppermint						✓	✓				
Spearmint						✓					
Uva Ursi				✓							✓

IMMUNE SYSTEM DISEASES/DISORDERS

	Chickenpox	Chills	Fever	Fungal infection	Lupus	Measles	Mononucleosis	Parasitic infection	Swollen lymph nodes	Yeast infection				
Catnip		✓	✓											
Chamomile					✓									
Cinnamon										✓				
Cleavers	✓		✓			✓	✓							
Echinacea			✓	✓				✓		✓				
Ginger								✓						
Lemon Grass		✓												
Licorice					✓									
Rosemary										✓				

MISCELLANEOUS DISEASES/DISORDERS

	Anemia	Cancer	Headache	Hemorrhage	Hirsutism	Hyperthyroidism	Obesity	Shock
Dandelion	✓						✓	
Gingko		✓						
Ginseng		✓						✓
Goji Berry		✓						
Lavender			✓			✓		
Lemon Balm			✓					
Lemon Peel			✓					
Licorice		✓						
Nettle	✓			✓				
Parsley	✓							
Passion Flower			✓					
Peppermint			✓					
Rosemary		✓	✓					
Spearmint			✓		✓			
Skullcap			✓					

MUSCULOSKELETAL DISEASES/DISORDERS

	Arthritis	Muscle aches	Osteoarthritis	Rheumatism	Rheumatoid arthritis
Chamomile	✓				
Dandelion				✓	
Licorice					✓
Nettle			✓		✓
Parsley	✓				
Rose Hips			✓		✓
Rosemary		✓		✓	
Uva Ursi	✓				
Wild Yam				✓	

NEUROLOGICAL DISEASES/DISORDERS

	Alzheimer's disease	Anxiety	Attention deficit disorder	Depression	Epilepsy	Hysteria	Insomnia	Irritability	Memory loss	Migraine	Nervousness	Neuralgia	Restless legs	Stress
Catnip							✓				✓			
Chamomile		✓					✓							✓
Cleavers							✓							
Cramp Bark											✓			
Gingko	✓		✓	✓					✓					
Ginseng		✓					✓							✓
Hops		✓					✓	✓						✓
Lavender		✓					✓			✓	✓			
Lemon Balm		✓		✓			✓				✓			
Lemon Grass		✓												
Passion Flower		✓			✓	✓	✓	✓					✓	✓
Peppermint							✓							
Rosemary		✓		✓										
Spearmint												✓		
Skullcap				✓			✓	✓				✓	✓	
Wild Yam												✓		

REPRODUCTIVE DISEASES/DISORDERS

	Heavy menstrual bleeding	Increases flow of breast milk	Impotence	Infertility	Labor pain	Menopause symptoms	Menstrual cramps	Miscarriage, threatened	Morning sickness	Pelvic inflammatory disease	Premenstrual syndrome		
Chamomile											✓		
Cinnamon							✓						
Cramp Bark							✓						
Corn Silk											✓		
Dandelion											✓		
Ginseng			✓	✓									
Goldenseal							✓			✓			
Milk Thistle		✓											
Nettle	✓	✓											
Parsley	✓						✓						
Passion Flower											✓		
Peppermint									✓				
Uva Ursi	✓												
Wild Yam					✓	✓	✓	✓					

RESPIRATORY TRACT DISEASES/DISORDERS

	Allergic rhinitis	Allergies	Asthma	Bronchitis	Chest infection	Colds	Coughs	Ear infections	Flu	Sore throat	Tonsillitis	Upper respiratory tract infection
Catnip						✓			✓			
Cayenne						✓						
Chamomile		✓	✓									
Cinnamon						✓			✓			
Cleavers											✓	
Cramp Bark			✓									
Echinacea					✓	✓	✓	✓	✓	✓		
Fennel		✓					✓					
Ginger		✓	✓			✓	✓		✓			
Gingko			✓									
Hibiscus												✓
Lavender						✓	✓					
Lemon Balm						✓			✓			
Lemon Peel						✓						
Licorice		✓	✓	✓			✓					
Marshmallow				✓			✓					
Nettle	✓		✓			✓						
Orange Peel						✓	✓					
Passion Flower			✓									
Peppermint						✓			✓			
Rose Hips						✓			✓			
Spearmint						✓				✓		
Slippery elm				✓			✓					
Uva ursi				✓								

SKIN DISEASES/DISORDERS

	Acne	Dermatitis	Eczema	General skin disorders	Hives	Psoriasis	Shingles	Ulcers
Cayenne								✓
Chamomile					✓	✓		
Cranberry								✓
Dandelion	✓		✓			✓		
Fennel		✓						
Goldenseal				✓				✓
Milk thistle	✓					✓		
Passionflower							✓	
Rosemary			✓					

URINARY TRACT DISEASES/DISORDERS

	Bloating	Edema	Enuresis	Gout	Incontinence	Kidney disease	Kidney stones	Prostatitis	Urethritis	Urinary tract infection
Cleavers	✓	✓					✓			✓
Cranberry					✓		✓			✓
Corn Silk	✓	✓	✓				✓		✓	✓
Dandelion				✓						✓
Fennel										✓
Hibiscus	✓									
Marshmallow							✓		✓	✓
Nettle					✓					✓
Parsley		✓		✓			✓			✓
Uva Ursi	✓					✓		✓		✓

References

Balch, P. (2002). *Prescription for Herbal Healing*. New York: Penguin Putnam, Inc.

Brown, D (2001). *Encyclopedia of Herbs*. New York: DK Publishing, Inc.

Dean Coleman Herbal Luxuries. (2007, August 21). *Lemongrass-Uses and Benefits*. Retrieved June 1, 2011, from http://deancoleman.wordpress.com/2007/8/21/lemongrass

Drugs.com. *Catnip*. Retrieved May 31, 2011, from http://www.drugs.com/npp/catnip.html

Drugs.com. *Nutmeg*. Retrieved April 11, 2011, from http://www.drugs.com/npp/nutmeg.html

Emedicine health. *Allspice*. Retrieved May 31, 2011, from http://www.emedicinehealth.com/allspice

Fiedler, C (2009). *The Complete Idiot's Guide to Natural Remedies*. Indianapolis, IN: Penguin Group Inc.

Gaby, A., Batz, F., Chester, R., Constantine, G. (2006). *A-Z guide to drug-herb-vitamin Interactions*. New York: Three Rivers Press.

Herbs2000.com. *Cleavers*. Retrieved April 11, 2011, from http://www.herbs2000.com/herb/herbs_cleavers.htm

Jacobs, B. (1981). *Growing and Using Herbs Successfully*. North Adams, MA: Storey Publishing.

Mabey, R., McIntyre, M., Michael, P., Duff, G., Stevens, J. (1988). *The New Age Herbalist*. New York: Simon and Schuster.

Monterey Bay Spice Company. *Cornsilk, c/s*. Retrieved April 12, 2011, from http://www.herbco.com/p-915-cornsilk-cs.aspx

The Goji Juice Guide. *Goji Juice*. Retrieved March 8, 2011, from http://www.gojiguide.com/goji_berry.htm

University of Maryland Medical Center. *Milk Thistle*. Retrieved April 24, 2011, from http://www.umm.edu/altmed/articles/milk-thistle

University of Maryland Medical Center. *Passionflower*. Retrieved April 24, 2011, from http://www.umm.edu/altmed/articles/passionflower

University of Maryland Medical Center. *Skullcap*. Retrieved April 15, 2011, from http://www.umm.edu/altmed/articles/skullcap

University of Maryland Medical Center. *Stinging Nettle*. Retrieved April 24, 2011, from http://www.umm.edu/altmed/articles/stinging-nettle

University of Maryland Medical Center. *Wild Yam*. Retrieved May 31, 2011, from http://www.umm.edu/altmed/articles/wildyam

WebMD. *Allspice*. Retrieved May 13, 2011, from http://www.webmd.com/vitamins-supplements

WebMD. *Goji Berries: Health Benefits and Side Effects*. Retrieved May 31, 2011, from http://www.webmd.com/balance/goji-berries-health-benefits

WebMD. *Hibiscus*. Retrieved June 1, 2011, from http://www.webmd.com/vitamins-supplements/ingredient

Wikipedia. *Allspice*. Retrieved April 11, 2011, from http://en.wikipedia.org/wiki/Allspice

Wikipedia. *Althaea officinalis*. Retrieved May 31, 2011, from http://en.wikipedia.org/wiki/Althaea_officinalis

Wikipedia. *Cayenne pepper*. Retrieved April 12, 2011, from http://en.wikipedia.org/wiki/Cayenne_pepper

Wikipedia. *Cinnamon*. Retrieved April 11, 2011, from http://en.wikipedia.org/wiki/Cinnamon

Wikipedia. *Clove*. Retrieved April 12, 2011, from http://en.wikipedia.org/wiki/Clove

Wikipedia. *Comfrey*. Retrieved April 12, 2011, from http://en.wikipedia.org/wiki/Comfrey

Wikipedia. *Cranberry*. Retrieved April 12, 2011, from http://en.wikipedia.org/wiki/Cranberry

Wikipedia. *Cymbopogon*. Retrieved June 1, 2011, from http://en.wikipedia.org/wiki/Cymbopogon

Wikipedia. *Dioscorea villosa*. Retrieved May 31, 2011, from http://en.wikipedia.org/wiki/Dioscorea_villosa

Wikipedia. *Echinacea*. Retrieved June 1, 2011, from http://en.wikipedia.org/wiki/Echinacea

Wikipedia. *Fennel*. Retrieved June 1, 2011, from http://en.wikipedia.org/wiki/Fennel

Wikipedia. *Ginger*. Retrieved June 1, 2011, from http://en.wikipedia.org/wiki/Ginger

Wikipedia. *Gingko biloba*. Retrieved May 31, 2011, from http://en.wikipedia.org/wiki/Gingko_biloba

Wikipedia. *Ginseng*. Retrieved May 31, 2011, from http://en.wikipedia.org/wiki/Ginseng

Wikipedia. *Goldenseal*. Retrieved May 12, 2011, from http://en.wikipedia.org/wiki/Goldenseal

Wikipedia. *Hibiscus*. Retrieved May 12, 2011, from http://en.wikipedia.org/wiki/Hibiscus

Wikipedia. *Hops*. Retrieved May 12, 2011, from http://en.wikipedia.org/wiki/Hops

Wikipedia. *Lavender*. Retrieved May 12, 2011, from http://en.wikipedia.org/wiki/Lavender

Wikipedia. *Lemon*. Retrieved July 1, 2011, from http://en.wikipedia.org/wiki/Lemon

Wikipedia. *Liquorice*. Retrieved May 26, 2011, from http://en.wikipedia.org/wiki/Liquorice

Wikipedia. *Melissa officinalis*. Retrieved May 13, 2011, from http://en/wikipedia.org/wiki/Melissa_officinalis

Wikipedia. *Milk Thistle*. Retrieved April 24, 2011, from http://en.wikipedia.org/wiki/Milk_thistle

Wikipedia. *Nepeta*. Retrieved April 11, 2011, from http://en/wikipedia.org/wiki/Nepeta

Wikipedia. *Nutmeg*. Retrieved April 11, 2011, from http://en.wikipedia.org.wiki/Nutmeg

Wikipedia. *Orange*. Retrieved April 25, 2011, from http://en/wikipedia.org/wiki/Orange_fruit

Wikipedia. *Parsley*. Retrieved April 24, 2011, from http://en.wikipedia.org/wiki/Parsley

Wikipedia. *Skullcap*. Retrieved April 15, 2011, from http://en/wikipedia.org/wiki/Skullcap

Wikipedia. *Stinging Nettle*. Retrieved April 24, 2011, from http://en.wikipedia.org/wiki/Stinging_nettle

Wikipedia. *Taraxacum*. Retrieved April 12, 2011, from http://en.wikipedia.org/wiki/Taraxacum

Wikipedia. *Viburnum opulus*. Retrieved April 12, 2011, from http://en/wikipedia.org/wiki/Viburnum_opulus

Wikipedia. *Wolfberry*. Retrieved April 12, 2011, from http://en/wikipedia.org/wiki/Wolfberry

Index

5-HTP, 62
abdominal pain, 36
abrasions, 24, 79
abscesses, 59, 78
absinthe, 38
Accupril, 33, 103
ACE inhibitors, 62, 103
acetaminophen, 48, 61, 103
acetylcholine, 62
acidic, 31, 68, 79
acne, 27, 35, 36, 61
actinidine, 21
adaptogen, 43, 44, 57, 95
adaptogenic, 12, 99
alcohol, 24, 76, 103
alcoholism, 61
alkaloids, 33, 60, 68, 81
alkanes, 27
alkylamides, 36
allantoin, 33, 79
allergic rhinitis, 62
allergies, 24, 40, 45, 58, 66
allspice, 19, 92, 93, 103, 104, 105, 110, 123
alpha-linolenic acid, 44
alpha-terpinene, 56
alterative, 27, 36, 46
alzheimer's disease, 41, 117
amino acids, 39, 44, 50, 57
Aminophylline, 79, 103
analgesic, 24, 29, 39, 55, 76
anaphylaxis, 36
anemia, 35, 58, 62, 67
anesthesia, 36, 40, 61, 104
anesthetic, 20, 69, 79
anethole, 25, 38, 57
annual, 24, 27, 28, 48
antacids, 35, 103
anthelmintic, 29
anthocyanins, 71
antibacterial, 13, 21, 22, 23, 24, 29, 31, 36, 38, 39, 41, 44, 46, 48, 50, 52, 53, 55, 56, 57, 69, 73, 76, 79, 86, 87
anticarcinogenic, 31, 76
anticatarrhal, 46
anticonvulsant, 76
antidepressant, 52, 68
antidepressants, 24, 43, 103
antifungal, 21, 29, 41, 44, 55, 73, 75
antihistamine, 24
anti-inflammatory, 11, 23, 24, 27, 29, 35, 36, 39, 43, 44, 46, 50, 52, 57, 59, 68, 69, 71, 81, 86, 87, 92
antimicrobial, 19, 20, 25
antioxidant, 13, 20, 24, 25, 29, 31, 36, 41, 43, 44, 53, 56, 65, 66, 71, 73, 75, 76
anti-parasitic, 69
antipyretic, 39, 55
antiseptic, 13, 20, 29, 46, 56

antispasmodic, 13, 24, 27, 30, 38, 52, 53, 57, 69, 73, 81
antiviral, 36, 46, 53, 57, 76
anxiety, 24, 43, 50, 52, 53, 68, 73, 117
aperient, 27
aphrodisiac, 43
apigenin, 66
apiole, 66
apiolin, 66
arbutin, 79
aromatic, 29, 55
arthritis, 21, 23, 26, 55, 58, 62, 67, 71, 73, 75, 79, 81, 97, 116
asparagin, 50, 59
asparagines, 34, 57
asperuloside, 27
aspirin, 11, 20, 23, 29, 32, 40, 41, 43, 58, 62, 103
asthma, 24, 30, 36, 38, 40, 41, 58, 62, 68, 70
astringent, 13, 25, 27, 29, 30, 41, 46, 55, 56, 62, 64, 71, 78, 79
atherosclerosis, 24, 32
athlete's foot, 55
Atropine, 79, 103
attention deficit disorder, 41
azulenes, 69
balsam of Tolu, 26
barbituates, 24, 53, 76, 103
bedstraw, 27
berberine, 46
beta blockers, 62, 103
beta-elemene, 76
betaine, 36, 57
biennial, 66
bilobalides, 41
bioflavonoids, 56
birth control pills, 61, 81
bisabolol, 24
bitter, 13, 24, 27, 30, 36, 46, 49, 50, 55, 61, 64, 66, 68, 69, 76
bloating, 33, 48, 79
boils, 33, 59, 78
borneol, 64, 73
breast feeding, 20
breast lumps, benign, 27
breast milk, 14, 37, 61, 62, 118
bronchitis, 58, 59, 78, 79
bruises, 68
burns, 24, 52, 62, 78
bursitis, 23
Buspirone, 64, 103
caffeoyl, 36
caftaric acid, 36
calcium, 25, 31, 33, 34, 38, 43, 44, 56, 65, 66
calcium channel blockers, 62, 103
calcium oxylate, 25
camphor, 21, 52
canadine, 46

cancer, 13, 29, 41, 43, 45, 58, 61, 73, 113
capsaicin, 23
Cardec DM, 79, 103
cardiac glycosides, 46
cardiovascular disease, 45
carminative, 13, 20, 21, 25, 29, 38, 39, 52, 53, 55, 64, 65, 75, 81
carotenoids, 23, 35, 69, 71
carvacrol, 21
carvone, 75
caryophyllene, 20, 25, 28, 53
catechins, 71
catnip, 20, 21, 88, 96, 110, 114, 117, 119, 123
cayenne pepper, 22, 89, 103, 104, 105, 123
Celicard, 65, 103
chamazulene, 24
chamomile, 15, 23, 24, 35, 87, 88, 90, 91, 96, 97, 103, 104, 105, 109, 110, 111, 112, 114, 116, 117, 118, 119, 120
chemotherapy drugs, 36, 40, 61, 103
chest infections, 20
chickenpox, 27
chills, 23
chlorophyll, 27, 62
choline, 34, 43, 57, 69
chrysin, 24, 68
cichoric acid, 36
cineole, 20, 52, 73
cinnamaldehyde, 25
cinnamate, 25
cinnamon, 25, 88, 89, 98, 109, 110, 111, 114, 118, 119, 123
Cipro. *See* Ciprofloxacin
Ciprofloxacin, 35, 38, 103
cirrhosis, 33, 61
Cisapride, 70, 103
Cisplatin, 24, 36, 40, 61, 103
Citalopram, 41, 103
citral, 53, 54, 55, 56, 65
citric acid, 27, 48, 56, 71
citronellal, 21, 53, 54, 55
cleavers, 26, 27, 85, 104, 105, 109, 113, 114, 117, 119, 120, 121, 123
Clofibrate, 61, 103
clove, 19, 28, 29, 92, 103, 104, 105, 110, 111, 123
cnicine, 60
Coedine, 79, 103
colds, 10, 21, 23, 26, 36, 40, 52, 53, 56, 62, 65, 70, 71, 75, 87, 98, 119
colic, 21, 24, 30, 38, 40, 58, 64, 70, 75, 81
colitis, 46, 59, 78
comfrey, 12
confusion, 76
conjunctivitis, 46
constipation, 30, 35, 48, 59, 62, 110
convulsions, 12, 64
cooling, 27, 33, 35, 53, 55
copper, 43, 44
cornsilk, 32, 33, 93, 103, 123
corticosteroids, 58, 103
cough, 36, 38, 40, 52, 58, 59, 65, 78, 119
Coumadin. See Warfarin

coumarin, 25, 27, 30, 52, 56, 57, 68
cramp bark, 29, 86, 109, 110, 117, 118, 119
cranberry, 30, 31, 71, 93, 101, 103, 104, 105, 112, 121, 124
craneberry, 31
crategolic acid, 28
Crohn's disease, 50, 58, 81, 110
cuts, 24, 27, 68, 79
cyanidin, 48
Cyclophosphamide, 24, 36, 40, 103
Cyclosporine, 41, 103
cystine, 44
cystitis, 27, 59
dandelion, 12, 34, 35, 85, 92, 103, 104, 105, 110, 113, 115, 116, 118, 120, 121
dandruff, 73
deciduous, 30, 41, 78
decongestant, 46, 69
delphinidin, 48
dementia, 41, 97
demulcent, 59, 78
deodorant, 20, 52
Depakote, 76, 103
depression, 41, 50, 53, 73, 76, 117
dermatitis, 24, 38, 50
diabetes, 41, 43, 45, 58, 59, 61, 79
diaper rash, 24
diaphoretic, 27
diarrhea, 12, 20, 21, 26, 40, 41, 43, 55, 61, 62, 71, 75, 78, 110
Diazepam, 24, 64, 103
Diclofenac, 62, 103
digestive aid, 23, 35, 52, 53, 86
Digitalis, 11, 43
Digoxin, 12, 58, 103
Dilantin, 76, 103
dimethylvinyl carbinol, 49, 50
dioecious, 63
diosgenin, 80
diosmin, 73
diterpenes, 76
diuretic, 12, 14, 27, 30, 33, 34, 35, 38, 48, 50, 52, 56, 59, 61, 62, 66, 71, 79, 81, 85, 92
diuretics, 12, 27, 35, 41, 58, 62, 79, 93, 104, 105
diverticulitis, 78, 81
dizziness, 36, 41, 64, 76
Docetaxel, 24, 36, 40, 103
Doxycycline, 46, 103
ear infection, 36
echinacea, 35, 36, 94, 98, 103, 104, 114, 119, 124
echinosides, 36
Econazole, 36, 103
eczema, 24, 27, 35, 46, 50, 58, 59, 62, 64, 73
edema, 27, 33, 58, 67
emmenagogue, 46, 66
emollient, 59
enuresis, 33
enzymes, 68
Ephedrine, 79, 103
epilepsy, 68
essential fatty acids, 71
essential oils, 25, 36, 54, 60, 79

Etodolac, 58, 103
eucalyptol, 69
eugenol, 19, 20, 25, 28, 29, 53, 64
evergreen, 19, 25, 27, 28, 31, 63, 65, 73, 79
expectorant, 39, 57, 59
eye disorders, 41, 45
fats, 33, 39, 43, 50
febrifuge, 21, 27, 56
fennel, 37, 86, 103, 109, 110, 112, 119, 121, 124
fever, 13, 14, 21, 27, 36
Fexofenadine, 65, 103
fiber, 31
flatulence, 13, 20, 21, 23, 26, 38, 40, 52, 53, 55, 64, 65, 70, 73, 75, 81, 110
flavonoids, 23, 27, 28, 31, 36, 38, 52, 53, 57, 60, 66, 68, 69, 71, 79
flu, 21, 26, 40, 53, 70, 71, 87, 98
Flunitrazepam, 64, 103
Fluorouracil, 24, 36, 40, 104
Fluoxetine, 41, 104
Fluvoxamine, 41, 104
food poisoning, 29, 38, 86, 110
formic acid, 62
foxglove, 11
Fragmin, 20, 29, 43, 104
fungal infection, 36
Furosemide, 34, 35
galitannic acid, 27
gallbladder disease, 35
gallic acid, 79
gallotannic acid, 28
gallstones, 33, 40, 52, 70, 75
gangrene, 59
gastritis, 46, 59
gastroenteritis, 59
gastroesophageal reflux disease, 79
geraniol, 21, 53
ginger, 39, 40, 85, 86, 89, 97, 98, 103, 104, 105, 109, 110, 111, 112, 114, 119, 124
gingerols, 39
gingivitis, 32, 56, 59
gingko, 40, 41, 97, 99, 103, 104, 105, 109, 112, 113, 115, 117, 119, 124
ginkgolide, 41
ginseng, 42, 43, 89, 95, 103, 104, 105, 109, 113, 115, 117, 118, 124
ginsenosides, 42
glaucoma, 38, 53
Glimepiride, 41, 104
Glipizide, 41, 104
glucoquinones, 62
glucosides, 27
Glyburide, 41, 104
glycosides, 11, 20, 24, 33, 34, 36, 41, 48, 50, 76, 79, 103
glycyrrhizin, 57
goji berry, 44, 91, 101, 105, 109, 112, 113, 115, 123
goldenseal, 45, 46, 87, 94, 99, 103, 104, 105, 110, 112, 113, 118, 124
gout, 35, 53, 62, 67
gums, 20, 25, 33, 57, 68
halitosis, 26
hallucinations, 64
Haloperidol, 41, 61, 104
headache, 21, 41, 43, 52, 53, 55, 64, 68, 70, 73, 75, 76, 115
heart attack, 12, 41, 43
heart disease, 12
heavy menstrual bleeding, 26, 62, 79
hemiarin, 52
hemorrhage, 62
hemorrhoids, 21, 62, 79
heparin, 20, 23, 29, 40, 41, 43, 46, 104
hepatic, 46
hepatitis, 27, 33, 58, 61, 70
herbaceous, 49, 57, 62, 66, 69, 75, 76
herpes, 36, 50, 53, 58
hiatal hernia, 59
hibiscus, 47, 95, 96, 97, 103, 109, 110, 111, 119, 121, 123, 124
high blood pressure, 12, *See* hypertension
high cholesterol, 23, 40, 48, 55, 61, 65
hirsutism, 75
histamine, 13, 62
hives, 24
hops, 49, 88, 110, 117, 124
hordenine, 33
humulene, 21
hydrastine, 46
hydroquinones, 30, 79
hypertension, 23, 26, 27, 30, 33, 38, 41, 43, 46, 48, 58, 62, 65, 68
hyperthyroidism, 53
hypothyroidism, 58
hysteria, 68
ibuprofen, 58, 104
ileitis, 58
immunosuppressants, 36, 104
impotence, 43
incontinence, 32
indigestion, 20, 38, 40, 50, 53, 58, 64, 65, 70, 73, 75, 78, 110
infertility, 43
inflammation, 13, 40, 46, 118
inflammatory bowel disease, 40
insect bites, 29, 52, 53, 59, 62
insect repellant, 21, 53, 55, 70
insomnia, 21, 24, 27, 43, 50, 52, 53, 68, 70, 76, 88, 90, 117
Interferon, 58, 104
intermittent claudication, 41
intestinal parasites, 29
inulin, 34, 36
iridoids, 21
iron, 20, 34, 43, 44, 62, 65, 66
irritability, 52, 68, 76
irritable bowel syndrome, 24, 30, 38, 50, 53, 58, 59, 70, 75, 78, 81
isoflavonoids, 57
Isoniazid, 58, 104
Ivermectin, 65, 104
jaundice, 61
karkade, 47
kidney disease, 12, 58, 62, 79

kidney stones, 27, 32, 33, 59, 67, 121
kinnikinnick, 79
labor pain, 81
Lansoprazole, 32, 104
Lasix. *See* Furosemide
lauric acid, 64
lavender, 51, 52, 91, 110, 111, 115, 117, 119, 124
lavendulyl acetate, 52
laxative, 13, 14, 27, 35, 46, 48, 57, 71, 78, 85
leaky gut syndrome, 58
lemon, 56
lemon balm, 52, 53, 90, 91, 95, 96, 105, 110, 115, 117, 119
lemon grass, 54, 55, 87, 96, 109, 110, 111, 114, 117
lemon peel, 55, 96, 110, 112, 115, 119
lice, 55
licorice, 12, 57, 85, 89, 103, 104, 105, 110, 111, 112, 113, 114, 115, 116, 119
limonene, 52, 56, 65, 69, 75
linalool, 25, 52, 73
linalyl acetate, 53
linoleic acid, 38, 60, 64
Lithium, 35, 104
liver disorders, 35, 38, 46
Lomotil, 79, 104
Lonox, 79, 104
Lorazepam, 24, 104
loss of appetite, 48
Lovastatin, 61, 104
Lovenox, 20, 29, 43, 104
low sex drive, 68
lupus, 24, 58
lutein, 31, 44
lycopene, 44
mace, 63
magnesium, 20, 31, 43, 65
maleic acid, 48
malic acid, 31, 71
maltol, 68
manganese, 20, 23, 31, 34, 43, 44, 62, 66
MAOIs, 41, 43, 68, 104
marshmallow, 58, 59, 86, 88, 89, 90, 93, 110, 111, 119, 121
mastitis, 24, 59
measles, 27
memory loss, 41, 117
Meniere's disease, 46, 58, 112
menopause, 81
menstrual cramps, 26, 30, 40, 46, 81, 118
menstrual disorders, 67
menthofuran, 69
menthol, 69
menthone, 69
menthylacetate, 69
Metformin, 41, 104
Methotrexate, 24, 36, 40, 61, 104
methyl salicylate, 28
Metronidazole, 61, 104
migraine, 52
milk thistle, 60, 92, 103, 104, 105, 109, 113, 118, 123, 124
minerals, 9, 39, 48, 62

miscarriage, 30, 81
mononucleosis, 27
Monterey Bay Spice Company, 15, 101, 123
morning sickness, 70
mosquito bites, 67
motion sickness, 24, 38, 40
mucilage, 25, 56, 59, 60, 77, 78, 86, 87, 93
mucilaginous, 59, 78
muscle aches, 20, 23, 30, 40, 52, 73, *116*
myrcene, 54, 55
myristic acid, 64
myristicin, 66
Nabumetone, 58, 104
Naproxen, 58, 104
narcotics, 24, 104
nardus, 51
nausea, 12, 23, 30, 36, 40, 41, 43, 52, 55, 62, 64, 70, 75, 86, 97, 98, 111
nepetalactone, 21
nepetol, 21
nerol, 21
nervine, 68, 76, 91, 95
nervousness, 21, 30, 52, 53, 54, 76
nettle, 61, 62, 85, 89, 103, 104, 105, 109, 110, 111, 115, 116, 118, 119, 121, 123, 124
neuralgia, 23, 55, 62, 70, 73, 75, 76, 81, 117
Nexium, 23, 104
nitrous oxide, 40, 61, 104
Normiflo, 20, 29, 43, 104
nosebleed, 43, 62
NSAIDS, 20, 29, 43, 62, 104
nutmeg, 19, 63, 64, 88, 103, 104, 110, 111, 123, 124
obesity, 35
oleic acid, 38, 64
oleoresin, 39
Omeprazole, 32, 104
Ondansetron, 64, 104
orange peel, 64, 65, 87, 90, 95, 103, 104, 105, 109, 110, 119
organic acids, 48, 68
Orgaran, 20, 29, 43, 104
osteoarthritis, 62, 71
Oxaprozin, 58, 104
oxytocic, 46
Paclitaxel, 24, 36, 40, 61, 104
palmitic acid, 64
pancreatitis, 79
parasitic infection, 36, 40
Paroxetine, 41, 104
parsley, 66, 93, 115, 116, 118, 121, 124
passionflower, 67, 68, 88, 89, 97, 99, 104, 123
pectin, 34, 43, 56, 71
pelvic inflammatory disease, 46
pemmican, 31
Pepcid, 23, 104
peppermint, 69, 70, 86, 87, 94, 98, 99, 103, 105, 110, 111, 113, 115, 117, 118, 119
peptic ulcer, 29
perennial, 38, 39, 49, 51, 53, 57, 62, 69, 71, 73, 75, 76
periodontal disease, 46
pesticide, 69
phellandrene, 20, 75

phenobarbitol, 24, 104
phenolic acids, 34, 73
phenols, 36, 44
phosphorous, 31, 65, 66
phytoestrogen, 42, 50, 80
phytol, 69
phytosterols, 44, 68, 81
pinene, 52, 56, 66, 69
Plavix, 20, 62, 104
polyacetylenes, 36
polyphenolic acids, 27
polyphenols, 31, 53
polysaccharides, 24, 36, 44, 48
pomfrets, 57
poor circulation, 40, 73
potassium, 12, 20, 23, 31, 33, 34, 38, 44, 56, 58, 62, 65
Pravachol, 65, 104
Pravastatin, 61, 105
pregnancy, 20, 21, 24, 26, 27, 36, 38, 41, 43, 46, 48, 50, 52, 55, 58, 64, 67, 68, 73, 75, 76, 78, 79
premenstrual syndrome, 24, 33, 35, 68
Prilosec, 23, 105
progesterone, 80
Propulsid. See Cisapride
prostatitis, 79
protease inhibitors, 46, 105
protein, 39, 44
Pseudoephedrine, 79, 105
psoriasis, 23, 24, 27, 35, 36, 58, 59, 61, 120
pulegone, 69
pyrrolizioline alkaloids, 12
quercetin, 20
quinapril. *See* Accupril
quinoline antibiotics, 65, 105
rash, 36
relaxant, 14, 21, 30, 50, 52, 53, 68, 91, 95, 99
Repaglinide, 41, 105
resins, 20, 25, 30, 33, 36, 46, 49, 50, 79
restless legs, 68, 88
restlessness, 41, 43
rheumatism, 35, 40, 52, 64, 70, 73
riboflavin, 23
ringworm, 55, 70
Risperidone, 58, 105
Rolaids, 23, 105
rose hips, 15, 70, 71, 87, 110, 116, 119
rosemary, 72, 73, 92, 109, 110, 114, 115, 116, 117
rosmanicine, 73
rosmarinic acid, 53, 69
rubichloric acid, 27
salicin, 11
salicosides, 30
saponins, 33, 43, 57, 81
scabies, 55
scars, 71
sciatica, 55, 62
scopoletin, 30
sedative, 14, 21, 24, 30, 39, 46, 50, 52, 53, 55, 68, 76, 79, 87, 88, 96
selenium, 20, 44
serotonin, 62

Sertraline, 41, 105
sesquiterpenes, 20, 28, 36
shingles, 58, 68
shock, 43
shogaols, 39
sialagogue, 39
silica, 62
silymarin, 60
sinusitis, 70
skin disorders, 27, 35, 46, 50, 52, 75
skullcap, 75, 76, 91, 95, 103, 105, 115, 117, 123, 124
slippery elm, 77, 78, 86, 87, 110, 111, 119
slug repellant., 65
snakebite, 35, 36, 52, 120
sodium, 12, 31, 58
soothing, 78
sore throat, 36, 38, 58, 75, 78
sores, 33, 53, 75
spearmint, 69, 74, 75, 94, 99, 110, 111, 113, 115, 117, 119
Spironolactone, 27, 35, 79, 105
sprains, 40, 55
SSRIs, 41
starch, 27, 39, 43, 57, 78, 81
steroids, 43
sterols, 33, 34, 43, 57, 68, 71
stimulant, 14, 21, 23, 29, 39, 41, 43, 65, 66, 69, 75
stings, 52, 62
stress, 13, 14, 24, 43, 50, 68, 91, 95, 97
stroke, 41
sugars, 25, 34, 43, 57, 68
sulfur, 62
sunburn, 27
swollen lymph nodes, 27
Tacrine, 61, 105
Tagamet, 23, 105
tannic acid, 79
tannins, 20, 21, 24, 25, 27, 28, 30, 31, 33, 50, 52, 53, 59, 60, 69, 71, 76, 78, 79, 81
taraxacin, 34
tartaric acid, 48
tendonitis, 55
terpenes, 64
terpineol, 52, 64
Tetracycline, 46, 105
Theophylline, 23, 79, 105
thymol, 21
thyroid hormones, 53, 105
Ticlopidine, 40, 41, 105
tinnitus, 41
tocopherols, 69
tongue inflammation, 56
tonic, 14, 20, 27, 43, 50, 52, 57, 61, 62, 64, 68, 76, 85, 89, 99
tonsillitis, 27
toothache, 26, 29, 64
Trazodone, 41, 105
Triamterene, 27, 35, 79, 105
triterpenes, 34
triterpenic acids, 73
triterpenoids, 28, 52, 53
Tums, 23, 105

twitching, 76
ulcers, 23, 24, 26, 27, 32, 40, 46, 50, 58, 59, 78, 79
umbelliferone, 52
upper respiratory tract infections, 48, 70
urethritis, 33, 59
urinary tract infections, 10, 32, 33, 35, 62, 67, 79, 93
ursolic acid, 79
uva ursi, 78, 79, 93, 103, 104, 105, 110, 113, 116, 118, 119, 121
valerian, 21
valeric acid, 30
Valium, 76, 105
vanadium, 43
vanillin, 28
varicose veins, 41, 59
verbenol, 73
vertigo, 41
viburnin, 30
Vitamin A, 20, 23, 31, 33, 34, 39, 44, 56, 62, 65, 66, 71
Vitamin B, 20, 34, 39, 56, 65, 71
Vitamin B1, 43
Vitamin B12, 43
Vitamin B2, 43, 44
Vitamin B6, 23, 44
Vitamin C, 20, 22, 23, 27, 31, 33, 34, 44, 48, 56, 62, 65, 66, 71, 87

Vitamin D, 34
Vitamin E, 23, 36, 44, 71
Vitamin K, 31, 33, 34, 71
volatile oils, 9, 19, 24, 28, 33, 36, 38, 39, 43, 46, 50, 56, 57, 64, 69, 71, 76, 79
vomiting, 12, 14, 41, 55, 61, 64, 70, 75
vulnerary, 27, 59
Warfarin, 20, 23, 24, 29, 32, 40, 41, 43, 45, 46, 62, 105
warming, 14, 20, 25, 29, 39, 43, 64
water retention. *See* edema
wax, 57
weight loss, 48
white willow bark, 11
wild yam, 80, 81, 92, 110, 116, 117, 118, 123
wolfberries, 44
wounds, 14, 27, 36, 73, 78
wrinkles, 71
Xanax, 76, 105
yarrow, 35
yeast infections, 26, 36, 73
Zantac, 23, 105
zeaxanthin, 31, 44
zinc, 35, 43, 44, 65
zingerone, 39

Acknowledgements

Thanks to all of the following people for all their help and support with this book and Maria's Mixes, LLC. This book would not have been possible without all of your help!

Marian Yeager – for your support and editing!
Anna Sowa – for allowing me to make your wedding favors and for all the support and ideas in developing Maria's Mixes, LLC!
Mike Ortiz – for your ideas and support in developing Maria's Mixes, LLC!
Lauren Owens – for introducing me to Annie Hinton and supporting Maria's Mixes, LLC!
Annie Hinton – for allowing Maria's Mixes, LLC to supply Brady's Smile, Inc. with tea!
Anne-Kathleen Borushko – for allowing me to supply Maria's Mixes tea to Jefferson school!
Sharon Nagashima – for your support and ideas!

Photographic credits

Pgs. 8, 10 – Dave O via Flickr/Creative Commons Attribution-Share Alike, www.flickr.com/photos/uncleweed
Pg. 14 – Kamil Porembinski via Flickr/Creative Commons Attribution-Share Alike, www.flickr.com/photos/paszczak000
Pg. 15 – Michael Lehet vis Flickr/Creative Commons Attribution-no derivative works, www.flickr.com/photos/mlehet
Pg. 17 – Living in Monrovia via Flickr/Creative Commons Attribution-Share Alike, www.flickr.com/photos/livinginmonrovia
Pg. 18 – Ryan Snyder via Flickr/Creative Commons Attribution, www.flickr.com/photos/ryansnyder/2426054523
Pg. 19 – The County Clerk via Flickr/Creative Commons Attribution-Share Alike, www.fotopedia.com/items/flickr-2555988821
Pg. 21 – J. Chris Vaughan via Flickr/Creative Commons Attribution-Share Alike, www.flickr.com/photos/grumpychris
Pg. 24, 56 – Fotos Van Robin via Flickr/Creative Commons Attribution-Share Alike, www.flickr.com/photos/fotosvanrobin
Pg. 25 – Joost J. Bakker IJmuiden via Flickr/Creative Commons Attribution, www.flickr.com/photos/joost-ijmuiden/5658441544
Pg. 27 – EpSos de via Flickr/Creative Commons Attribution, www.flickr.com/photos/epsos
Pgs. 28, 85 – Leonora Enking via Flickr/Creative Commons Attribution-Share Alike, www.flickr.com/photos/33037892@N04
Pg. 30 – Andrew Yee via Flickr/Creative Commons Attribution, www.flickr.com/photos/halfchinese
Pg. 31 – Stereogab via Flickr/Creative Commons Attribution, www.flickr.com/photos/stereogab
Pg. 33 – marcu iocham via Foto Community/Creative Commons Attribution, www.fotocommunity.com/pc/pc/display/24479097
Pg. 34 – Jordan Neeter via Flickr/Creative Commons Attribution, www.flickr.com/photos/barefootgardener
Pg. 36 – Rowena via Flickr/Creative Commons Attribution-no derivative works, www.flickr.com/photos/rubber_slippers_in_italy
Pg. 38 – Delphine Menard via Flickr/Creative Commons Attribution-Share Alike, www.flickr.com/photos/notafish
Pg. 39 - Anders Sandberg via Flickr/Creative Commons Attribution, www.flickr.com/photos/arenamontanus
Pg. 41 – Chloester via Flickr/Creative Commons Attribution-Share Alike, www.flickr.com/photos/etherealdawn
Pg. 43 – Daveeza via Flickr/Creative Commons Attribution-Share Alike, www.flickr.com/photos/vizpix
Pg. 44 – Keith Robinson via Flickr/Creative Commons Attribution-no derivative works, www.flickr.com/photos/kjrob
Pg. 46 – Tom Raftery via Flickr/Creative Commons Attribution-Share Alike, www.flickr.com/photos/traftery
Pg. 48 – NZ Craft Beer TV via Flickr/Creative Commons Attribution, www.flickr.com/photos/nzcraftbeertv
Pg. 50 – Limbo Poet via Flickr/Creative Commons Attribution, www.flickr.com/photos/44639455@N00
Pgs. 51, 87 – color line via Flickr/Creative Commons Attribution, www.flickr.com/photos/sunrise
Pg. 53 – Clay Irving via Flickr/Creative Commons Attribution-no derivative works, www.flickr.com/photos/clayirving
Pg. 54 – Alejandra Owens via Flickr/Creative Commons Attribution-no derivative works, www.flicker.com/photos/alejandraowens
Pg. 57 – Phil Sellens via Flickr/Creative Commons Attribution, www.flickr.com/photos/phil_sellens/3856431595
Pgs. 59, 90 – Andrew Bossi via Flickr/Creative Commons Attribution-Share Alike, www.flickr.com/photos/thisisbossi
Pg. 60 – Lauren Tucker via Flickr/Creative Commons Attribution-no derivative works, www.flickr.com/photos/photographygal
Pg. 62 – Ramesh NG via Flickr/Creative Commons Attribution-Share Alike, www.flilckr.com/photos/rameshng
Pg. 63 – Veganbaking.net via Flickr/Creative Commons Attribution-Share Alike, www.flickr.com/photos/vegan-baking
Pg. 65 – Hlijod Huskona via Flickr/Creative Commons Attribution-no derivative works, www.flickr.com/photos/lorelei-ranveig
Pg. 66 – Roy Niswanger via Flickr/Creative Commons Attribution-no derivative works, www.flilckr.com/photos/motleypixel
Pg. 68 - Til Westermayer via Flickr/Creative Commons Attribution-Share Alike, www.flilckr.com/photos/tilwe
Pg. 69 – cheekycrows3 via Flickr/Creative Commons Attribution-no derivative works, www.flickr.com/photos/sycamoremoonstudios
Pg. 71 – geishaboy500 via Flilckr/Creative Commons Attribution, www.flickr.com/photos/geishaboy500

Photographic credits, cont.

Pgs. 73, 92 – Quinn Dombrowski via Flickr/Creative Commons Attribution-Share Alike, www.flilckr.com/photos/quinnanya
Pg. 74 – U.S. Army Environmental Command via Flickr/Creative Commons Attribution, www.flickr.com/photos/armyenvironmental
Pg. 76 – Charl de Martigny via Flickr/Creative Commons Attribution, www.flickr.com/photos/demartigny
Pg. 77 – Cliff via Flickr/Creative Commons Attribution, www.flickr.com/photos/nostri-imago
Pg. 79 – Dave Bonta via Flickr/Creative Commons Attribution-Share Alike, www.flickr.com/photos/89056025
Pg. 81 – grendelkhan via Flickr/Creative Commons Attribution-Share Alike, www.flickr.com/photos/grendelkhan
Pg. 83 – Holy Outlaw via Flickr/Creative Commons Attribution-no derivative works, www.flickr.com/photos/holyoutlaw
Pg. 84 – heymrleej via Fotopedia/Creative Commons Attribution-Share Alike, www.fotopedia.com/items/flickr-3338424891
Pg. 86 – David Blaikie via Flickr/Creative Commons Attribution, www.flickr.com/photos/nikonvscanon
Pg. 87 – Just started to learn/ReCreation via Flickr/Creative Commons Attribution-Share Alike, www.flickr.com/photos/recreation
Pg. 89 – Jack Wolf via Flickr/Creative Commons Attribution-no derivative works, www.flickr.com/photos/wolfraven
Pg. 91 – Rene Schwietzke via Flickr/Creative Commons Attribution, www.flickr.com/photos/rene-germany
Pg. 93 – umjanedoan via Flickr/Creative Commons Attribution, www.flickr.com/photos/umjanedoan
Pg. 94 – Lori Grieg via Flickr/Creative Commons Attribution-no derivative works, www.flickr.com/photos/lori_grieg
Pg. 95 – Flare via Flickr/Creative Commons Attribution-no derivative works, www.flickr.com/photos/75898532
Pg. 96 – Randy OHC via Flickr/Creative Commons Attribution, www.flickr.com/photos/mariya_umama_wethemba_mc
Pg. 97 – Rupert Ganzer via Flickr/Creative Commons Attribution, no derivative works, www.flickr.com/photos/loop_oh
Pg. 99 – Chris Gladis via Flickr/Creative Commons Attribution, no derivative works, www.flickr.com/photos/mshades
Pg.128 – Selena N.B.H. via Flickr/Creative Commons Attribution, www.flickr.com/photos/moonlightbulb

About the Author

Maria Yeager grew up in Cincinnati, Ohio. After graduating from Eastern Kentucky University with a B.S. in Microbiology and a Chemistry minor, she worked for 23 years as a laboratory technologist for several major U.S. labs. In 1996, she became certified as a Clinical Laboratory Specialist in Cytogenetics (CLspCG). Over the next few years, she had several health issues that failed to respond to medical treatment, and this propelled her into the study of alternative medicine. She received a Master's Degree in Holistic Nutrition from Clayton College of Natural Health and graduated with Highest Honors. She then completed the Family Herbalist Certificate at the same college, again receiving Highest Honors. Maria is an avid believer in the power of holistic nutrition and herbs, and her desire is to educate people everywhere on how to support your body and live at optimum health through the proper addition of vitamins, minerals, herbs and other nutritional supplements.

Photo by Selena N.BH. via Flickr/Creative Commons

Made in the USA
Monee, IL
21 December 2022

23269753R00077